LYMINGTON
The Sound of Success

Alan Brown

Front cover. *Lymington* in postwar condition crossing (Late D.T. Pye)

Plate 1. Classic Car Ferry — Classic Car! The shape of cars may change but the *Lymington* design goes on for ever. Loading at Lymington in the mid sixties.
(Alan Brown collection)

Foreword

"LYMINGTON   THE SOUND OF SUCCESS"

A new ferry arrives on the scene for the first time; "ugly, purely functional" shout the critics, while the owners and designers dream of a trouble free inauguration into the thankless task of keeping the public quietly on the move (in my days at sea the most hazardous cargo possible was the *passenger!!*). Very occasionally the behind-the-scenes crossed fingers are tighter than usual as the owners take a calculated risk on a revolutionary new design to improve the service and capture more trade.

The "Lymington / Sound of Sanda" was one of these 'purely functional' vessels, but with a difference; the relatively new double-ended car ferry arrangement was combined for the first time with a relatively new propulsion concept (Voith Schneider Propeller), thus attracting considerable media and public attention when she first appeared. Usually such vessels then go about their working lives with little attention from most men until the shipbreaker's torch arrives.

Not such a ship the "Lymington / Sound of Sanda", for 50 years later she still plies her regular crossings with exceptional reliability in all weather; not such a man Alan Brown who discovered the ship was not only a living part of our maritime history, but also had an interesting story waiting to be told. Alan's discovery of this untold story, as so often happens, came about by chance whilst researching his earlier books, such as his accounts of the previously unheralded 'Talisman' and the ill-fated 'Shanklin / Prince Ivanhoe'. The result — "Lymington - The Sound of Success" — an excellent account of this historic pioneer, takes us through all the formative embryonic stage, the difficult teething and adolescent stage and up to the present-day stately, reliable, mature stage of the ship's life.

As with any successful pioneer, others follow and Alan includes a voyage down the ship's family tree which is noteworthy in two respects. Firstly, the line is far from coming to an end as the new ships and propellers offer long-term reliability in this short-term disposable age. Indeed, no alternative system has been, or is about to be developed which in any way threatens the family line. Secondly, the ancestor is still very much with us 50-years on. Hence the timely introduction of Alan Brown's latest dive into the ferryman's history which so ably places on record this remarkable little ship's full story.

Partner
E.C.GOLDSWORTHY & CO.

Author's Preface

Ten years ago, when it became known I was writing a history of the Clyde diesel-electric paddler *Talisman* the general reaction was one of incredulity — *"Talisman? What is there to write about Talisman?"* In fact, there was a great deal to write about this unique vessel and following publication incredulity changed to astonishment. "I never realised *Talisman* was such an interesting ship" was a not uncommon response. History repeats itself. *"Lymington!* What is there to write about *Lymington?* She was only an old Isle of Wight car ferry". Exactly, but one worthy of an honourable place in the annals of British maritime history.

I must confess that I myself had not given *Lymington* a second thought until undertaking research into the three Portsmouth-Ryde motorships and in the process found myself sidetracked down 'Lymington Lane'. The further I wandered along this intriguing path the more fascinating it became until I felt compelled to explore it right to the end. On this journey I found myself inexorably drawn in other by-ways, all interlinked with the main track, and I gradually realised that *Lymington* could not be considered in isolation but only as part of a much wider vista. By adopting this approach I accept that I may have left myself open to the accusation "what has all this to do with *Lymington",* and if one takes a narrow and blinkered view there may be some substance in that charge. However, in reply, I would suggest that to fully appreciate the historic and technical significance of *Lymington* herself she must be portrayed as the centrepiece of a broad tapestry, having as a bold background the development of the Solent and Firth of Clyde ferry services, together with the evolution of that remarkable device, the Voith Schneider propeller.

This is what I have tried to achieve.

Plate 2. *Lymington* in final BR condition on passage. The hinged gangways connecting both sides of the promenade decks can be seen clearly in this view.
(John Hendy).

Plate 3. Before: *P.S. Solent* and towboats carry vehicular traffic to the island in a fashion which would cause the present D.O.T. officials to have a fit! (Bert Moody)

INTRODUCTION

On the 1st May 1938 the *MV Lymington,* the first Voith Schneider propelled vessel to enter service in this country, and the first double-ended Voith-Schneider propelled ferry in the world, made her maiden voyage on the Southern Railway's Lymington-Yarmouth passage between the mainland and the Isle of Wight. Now renamed *Sound of Sanda,* and employed on Western Ferries Firth of Clyde services, this historic vessel celebrates half a century of virtually continuous all year round service in 1988.

Already under consideration for preservation when her working life finally comes to an end, *Lymington* pioneered the now almost universal layout for vessels employed on river, lake, estuary and narrow sea channel passenger/vehicle ferry crossings — double ended for ease and quickness of loading and unloading, diesel engine driven Voith Schneider propellers, placed fore and aft, for unrivalled control and manoeuvrability, and passenger accommodation arranged to give an unrestricted roll on, roll off vehicle deck. All subsequent vessels of this type, from the magnificent new 'Saint' class ships on the Solent to the relatively diminutive and recently introduced 'Loch' class ferries serving the Scottish highlands and islands can trace their ancestry directly back to *Lymington.* Such vessels form an essential part of the country's transport system, and whilst they have never attained the popularity or interest accorded to the more glamorous pleasure steamer, the story of *Lymington* is as equally interesting, if not more so, than many better known ships.

Lymington cannot be considered in isolation, and the story encompasses not only the background of the Solent ferry services, from the tow-boat era to the present day, but also traces the development of the Voith Schneider propeller and recounts the efforts of one man to persuade British shipowners of its outstanding attractions. How right the *Lymington* concept was has been proved by the introduction, fifty years later, of vessels varying only in size and detail from her basic design parameters, and it is fitting that the *Lymington* story should be published to coincide with her 50th birthday anniversary.

Lymington is a particularly interesting and important landmark in the history of marine engineering progress, and the fact that she remains in active service, powered by her original Allen diesel engines, fifty years after her maiden voyage, is a remarkable tribute to her conception and design, and a credit to the workmanship and care given to her construction and operation.

Plate 4. And after! This early sixties shot of *Lymington* belies the fact that there was ever any other way of getting to the island from Lymington other than by car ferry! Not far away the evidence of former ways can be seen. (See plate 33). (Alan Brown collection)

ACKNOWLEDGEMENTS

In a work of this nature one is heavily dependent on co-operation and goodwill. Research can be an expensive, time consuming and frustrating business and is either enjoyable or depressing, depending to a large extent on whether the response is enthusiastic and helpful or frigid and evasive. On the whole it is the former, but regrettably there are always one or two exceptions..

One of the happiest aspects, when the work is finally completed, is to remember and acknowledge those whose enthusiasm, interest and assistance made it all possible. First and foremost, I am deeply indebted to Jonathan Mason and Steve Taylor, the E.C. Goldsworthy & Co. Partners, for their most willing co-operation and hospitality, and also to the late Captain Goldsworthy, founder of the firm.

I am also most grateful to Ray Butcher, the Terminal Supervisor at Gunwharf Road, Portsmouth, for his assistance and many kindnesses. The ever friendly welcomes by Alan Bradley, Western Ferries' Managing Director; Captains Ken MacArthur, Jim Wilson, James Addison, Tom McCutcheon, Alan Eadie, Allan McKeller; and engineers Angus McLean and Cameron McCutcheon, have been greatly appreciated. Eric Payne, of Ryde, has kindly placed his own records at my disposal, which have proved invaluable and saved a great deal of time.

Fred Howland, former chief engineer of *Lymington,* made me most welcome at his home, and was able to fill many gaps in the story. Others include Andrew Wilson, a director of Western Ferries; Dr John Mackett; Roger Silsbury; Tim Cooper; Nick Boycott; and Richard Newman (all associated with the Isle of Wight Steam Railway); Captain Morse; Sealink, Portsmouth; and J. Knowles (W.H. Allen). The Librarians of the Institute of Marine Engineers; Beaulieu Motor Museum; Mitchell Library, Glasgow; Public Library, Dumbarton; Isle of Wight County Library; College of Nautical Studies, Warsash; and Portsmouth City Library have all assisted in locating information. In particular, Mrs Wiggins, of the national Maritime Museum Library, set me off on the path which eventually led to the door of E.C. Goldsworthy & Co. The editors of the Lymington Times; and the Isle of Wight County Press have also been most helpful, and it is always a pleasure to visit Mr Michael Moss and his staff at the Glasgow University Archives.

Dr Joe McKendrick; Leslie Brown; Iain MacArthur; Graham Langmuir; Fergus Allan; Fiona McMurray (Denny Tank); Bert Moody; Ron Adams; Keith Adams; Bill Windibank; Ben Wales; Richard Keeping; John Hendy; John Innes; and Peter Smith have all assisted in various ways. To anyone whom I have inadvertently omitted to mention, I tender my apologies.

The majority of the drawings and data sheets, together with a number of photographs, have been supplied by E.C. Goldsworthy & Co. Others are from a variety of sources and collections, and all have been individually acknowledged wherever possible. I am particularly grateful to Ray Butcher for his help in this respect.

Finally, to my wife, Connie, for assistance with research, typing the manuscript, and offering suggestions (not always accepted!) for its improvement.

The Author

Alan Brown was born in Middlesbrough and commenced his career as an electrical engineering apprentice in Dorman Long's steelworks and a local shipyard. Subsequently specialising in electric motors and motor control systems he held supervisory, design and managerial positions before leaving industry to take up lecturing in a technical college.

His association with coastal passenger steamers dates back to the 1920's, when family holidays were spent on the Firth of Clyde. Thereafter in post-war days, he became acquainted with all the major pleasure steamer fleets, cross channel steamers and continental lake and river paddle steamers.

With the decline of the traditional pleasure steamer fleets his eyes turned to the equally rapidly dwindling coastal, estuarial and cross-river ferries, and found these much despised, workaday ships quite as fascinating as their more glamorous sisters.

He is now retired, and lives at the Cumbrian port of Silloth, still researching, studying and pursuing the more original and unusual in the field of vintage machinery and transport.

Plate 5. A new lease of life. *Sound of Sanda* celebrates her fiftieth birthday in 1988 and is still sailing.   (Alan Brown collection)

CHAPTER 1

THE BACKGROUND

Plate 6. An early paddle steamer and tow boat, loaded with horse and carriage, approaches Ryde pier. (Alan Brown collection)

Crossing the Solent

From the earliest days of steamships the three principal crossings of the Solent, that twenty mile stretch of sparkling salt water which separates the Isle of Wight from the mainland, have been, from east to west:

Portsmouth — Ryde
Southampon — Cowes
Lymington — Yarmouth

The first steamship to ply on any of these routes, the *PS Britannia,* commenced operation on 19 May 1817, making two return crossings between Portsmouth and Ryde each day. However, it would appear that she was ill-suited, both in build and power, to cope with the boisterous seas, strong currents and high winds which can be encountered even during a Solent summer, and after less than a month in service she was withdrawn. After this inauspicious start it is perhaps not surprising that the next venture was on the rather more sheltered route between Southampton and Cowes, where a thrice-daily summer only service was introduced on 24 July 1820 by the *PS Prince of Cobourg.* Following the success of the "Cobourg" steam was given a second chance on the Ryde run in 1825, when the *P.S. Union* inaugurated a regular summer service on 5 April. Finally, on the same date in 1830 the *P.S. Glasgow* initiated a regular sailing between Lymington and Yarmouth, although this only formed part of a longer route to either Southampton or Portsmouth with calls at Cowes and Ryde. *Prince of Cobourg, Union* and *Glasgow* established the regular use of steamships on these three principal crossings and not only effected a marked improvement in the carriage of passengers and goods on the routes, but also expedited the transport of livestock and wheeled vehicles to and from the island.

Terminal facilities were often primitive or inconveniently situated. For example, on the Southampton-Cowes run it was not until the Royal Pier at Southampton was opened in 1833 that passengers were enabled to embark or dis-embark without the necessity of having to be rowed between ship and shore, and then only at high water periods. Travellers using the Portsmouth to Ryde route were rather more fortunate, since piers at both places permitted a regular non-tidal service, while those favouring the western Solent crossing often experienced delays due to lack of water at Lymington Quay, or stress of weather at the exposed Yarmouth harbour. Over the years conditions did of course improve, with new piers being built at Old Portsmouth (Victoria Pier) in 1842, Portsea (Albert Pier) in 1846 and Southsea (Clarence Pier) in 1861. By 1861 pontoons were in use at Southampton (River Itchen) and Fountains Quay, Cowes, with the steamers calling at the Itchen pontoon before proceeding to the Royal Pier. The latter acquired its own pontoon in 1867 and in 1871 the London & South Western Railway extended its line to a terminal station on the pier itself.

The Lymington Railway Act of 1856 empowered the company to purchase the quay and to make arrangements with the steamer company concerning the provision of suitable facilities. At that time passengers not only had to be ferried in small boats to and from the steamers when tidal conditions prevented them from reaching the Quay, but even when it was possible to berth the limited space frequently meant having to tie-up alongside a timber or coal vessel discharging cargo, over which passengers had to scramble at some peril to themselves and their attire. Although the line opened in 1858 the Town Station was not completed until September 1860 and in the following year a new steamer jetty, extending well out into the river beyond the station, was constructed and immediately put into use. Even so, problems continued to be experienced, and at low water it was still necessary to ferry passengers down river to steamers unable to reach the jetty. On the island side the construction of a breakwater at Yarmouth harbour afforded extra protection and tidal restrictions were eliminated when the new pier opened in 1876.

Competition between companies serving the same route inevitably led to rationalisation and by 1865 the Southampton-Cowes service had become the monopoly of the grandiosely titled Southampton, Isle of Wight and South of England Royal Mail Steam Packet Company — now better known as Red Funnel Steamers. At Portsmouth, rival companies eventually combined to form the Port of Portsmouth & Ryde United Steam Packet Company and which by 1876 had become the sole operator on the Ryde route. Railway services in the Portsmouth area were provided by the London, Brighton & South Coast Railway from the east, and from the west by the London & South Western Railway, both companies sharing a joint line from Cosham to a common terminal station in Commercial Road, Portsmouth. In 1876 the line was extended to the new Portsmouth Harbour station and pier, to which the steamer services were immediately transferred. Under the circumstances, it is not surprising that the two railway companies, but in particular the London Brighton & South Coast, were now anxious to have the steamer services under their own direct control, since these were, in effect, merely an extension of their own system across the Solent to the Isle of Wight. After a futile attempt by the steamer company to bargain with the railways the latter took over the ships and assets of the Port of Portsmouth & Ryde United Steam Packet Company on 31 March 1880, and direct railway operation under the Joint Committee of the two companies commenced on the following day.

The London & South Western Railway, which had worked the Lymington Railway from its inception, purchased the line in 1879 and following the success of the Freshwater, Yarmouth & Newport Railway Act in 1880 the London & South Western Railway directors resolved to extend their line from Lymington Town station to a new combined station and pier further downstream, accessible at all states of the tide but on the opposite bank of the river. The new terminal, named Lymington Pier, opened to traffic on 1 May 1884, the line crossing the river immediately south of the town station by means of a 70 yard long single track viaduct. Four through-trains from Waterloo connected with the steamers daily, whilst livestock, vehicles and cargo were conveyed by a tow boat service leaving Lymington slipway daily at 11.00 am.

The steamers had for many years been owned and operated by the Solent Steam Packet Company, but following the extension of the line to Lymington Pier the railway company purchased from the Steam Packet Company the paddle steamers *Mayflower* and *Solent,* four tow boats and associated property for £2,750, and direct operation of the steamer service by the London & South Western Railway commenced on 1 July 1884. Thus commenced the hundred year era of railway operated shipping services on these two routes, which were to reach their zenith in the mid 'thirties during the halcyon days of Southern Railway ownership.

The Tow Boats

The use of tow boats for the transport of livestock and wheeled vehicles originated in 1825 on the Portsmouth-Ryde route when the *Union* and two small tow boats first entered service. The latter were advertised for "the conveyance of carriages, horses and cattle, which will be enabled to walk to and from the beach when shipped and landed". Six years later tow boats were introduced on the Southampton-Cowes run and Lymington finally followed suit in 1836. These heavily built, broad beamed, shallow draft craft were fitted with a flat, hinged stern door kept watertight by packing with sacking and pulled up tight with blocks and tackle. This stern door could be lowered to form a short loading ramp, although planks were always additionally used to bridge the gap between the boat and beach or slipway. Those employed on the Southampton-Cowes route — ever the odd man out — used bow ramps!

In the early days these boats, weather and tide permitting, were poled from a conveniently situated gently sloping beach out into the fairway and picked up by one of the passenger steamers on a service run. At the destination, the tow was released and the boat guided and poled, stern first, onto the shore, where the ramp was lowered and the livestock or vehicles disembarked; the pandemonium which ensued when herding cattle, sheep and other animals on and off the boats can be well imagined. Later, proper slipways were constructed, but whether using beaches or slipways great care had to be exercised by the boatmen during a falling tide to ensure that they did not become stranded.

On the Portsmouth-Ryde route a slipway at the end of Broad Street, Portsmouth Point, and usable at all states of the tide, formed the mainland terminal, whilst at Ryde the George Street slipway, east of Ryde pier and accessible at high water only was initially used. The Tramway pier, built alongside Ryde pier and opened in 1864, incorporated a slipway accessible at all states of the tide, which permitted a more flexible service to be provided but this slipway had to be demolished to facilitate construction of the new railway pier, to the east of the Tramway pier, in 1880 and the tow-boat service reverted to the tidal George Street slipway. A slipway adjacent to Lymington station formed the mainland terminal of the western Solent service whilst on the island landings were made at a short slipway alongside Yarmouth castle.

The use of passenger steamers on service runs for hauling the tow boats was not universally appreciated, since the practice resulted in delays and reduced the speed of the vessel whilst on passage, but the alternative was even worse! If stress of weather or other circumstances prevented the use of the tow boats passengers had then to share the deck of the steamer with cattle, sheep, horses and even pigs — circumstances not calculated to ensure a tranquil or enjoyable passage to those of genteel upbringing or a less than robust constitution. However, as early as 1850 an advertisement for the Portsmouth-Ryde service intimated that the tow boat service would run three times daily, but at different times to the passenger steamers, in order to avoid delays to the latter.

The deficiencies of the towboat services were recognised by a group of visionaries, sixty years or more ahead of their time, who, in 1860 introduced the paddle steamer *Victoria* on the Portsmouth-Ryde route. This remarkable vessel was in effect a steam powered tow boat, having the same hinged stern door and specifically designed for the carriage of livestock and vehicular traffic to and from the island. She was probably the first steam powered roll-on roll-off vessel to be used in England (*Leviathan*, the first roll-on roll-off train ferry in the world having entered service on the Edinburgh, Perth & Dundee Railway company's Granton — Burntisland service in 1849) and in addition had the honour of being the first vessel to be constructed at the Wallsend-on-Tyne yard of Wigham Richardson & Co. Although rather longer at 65ft than the contemporary tow boats little is known of her service on the route, but it may be that success eluded her due to encroachment of deck space by her machinery and boiler and it was not until 1927 that the experiment was repeated in a more versatile and up-to-date version.

The practice of using passenger steamers as towing vessels was gradually phased out and small steam screw tugs were either purchased or hired for this work, although on the Portsmouth service even a Gosport ferry was occasionally pressed into service if a tug was not available. The changeover took place around the turn of the century, subsequent to the railway takeover, but it was by no means unusual to find the reserve Lymington paddler deputising for a tug right up to the final days of the tow boats. Perhaps the best known of these tugs were the *Adur* and *Adur II* at Portsmouth — the former serving up to the demise of the tow boats on the route — and the twin screw *Carrier*, acquired by the London & South Western Railway in 1906, and based at Lymington, which also had a certificate for 290 passengers. Following *Carrier's* conversion to a barge around 1931 the stand-by paddle steamer *Solent* was used, and the steam tug *Jumsey* hired as and when necessary.

Plate 7. An aerial view of Lymington, showing the 1861 pier extending downstream just below the viaduct. Note the tug *Carrier* at the pier and a tow boat tied up to the left of *Carrier*. A further tow boat can be seen at the slipway/dock to the left of the first tow boat. The tow boat service operated from here as there were no loading facilities at Lymington Pier Station, towards which the railway line can be seen extending beyond the viaduct. Lymington Town Station is located mid-way between the viaduct and left edge of illustration.   (Alan Brown collection)

Plate 8. Unloading racehorses at George Street slipway, Ryde. The tug *Adur* with another towboat lies off.   R. Silsbury

Plate 9. A tug and towboat leaving George Street slipway, Ryde. Manoeuvering the towboats onto the slip under certain tidal and weather conditions could be very tricky.   (R. Butcher collection)

Plate 10. Loading at Lymington old slipway. Cars were backed onto the tow boats via two stout planks. The driver seems very confident on his reversing abilities! Unlike Ryde, at least there was a quay wall to warp the towboat alongside.   (Alan Brown collection)

Plate 11. An empty towboat at Lymington with *Carrier* in the background, at the 1861 pier. Note sailing ships at the Town Quay on the right.   (R. Coles collection)

Motor Car Traffic

The transport of motor vehicles by the tow boats seems to have commenced during the early years of the 20th century, and whilst the carriage of the first motor car on the Ryde route appears to have gone unrecorded it was the then Lord Montague of Beaulieu who made the earliest crossing on the Lymington-Yarmouth passage. By 1906 the London & South Western Railway felt that with the increasing popularity of motor touring in Hampshire and the Isle of Wight their facilities for the transport of motor cars to and from the island deserved more publicity. Although times of departure from Yarmouth at 8.15am and 1.30pm were quoted, and from Lymington at 11.30am the 'Hampshire Advertiser' in its issue of 21 April 1906 stressed that a tug (and presumably a tow boat) was available at all times for the conveyance of motor vehicles to and from the island at a small additional charge. In 1907 300 motor cars were conveyed between Lymington and Yarmouth and by 1913 the number had increased to almost 700, whilst in the year ending 31 May 1925 the cars handled had again almost doubled to 1,269. Thereafter the number continued to steadily increase until in 1937, the last full year of tow-boat operation, the figure stood at 2,447. Motor vehicle traffic continued to flourish likewise on the other routes in spite of the primitive, tedious and often inconveniently timed crossings to Ryde, where arrivals and departures were restricted to times coinciding with half an hour before high water in order to avoid a long and hazardous drive over an expanse of wet sand. Motorists were certainly better catered for on the Cowes run since the provision of pontoons at Southampton and Cowes permitted cars to be side-loaded onto the foredeck of the paddle steamers at all times. Even so, in the early 'twenties both the Southampton company and the Southern Railway were increasingly criticised for their apparent indifference to the needs of motorists, which in the case of the railway company was perhaps only to be expected, since every motor vehicle carried represented a potential loss of rail traffic. In spite of this they adopted a remarkably enlightened attitude towards the motorist and one of the earliest tasks of the Southern

management was to investigate sites in the vicinity of Ryde which would enable them to operate a regular, non-tidal tow boat service. The most suitable location was considered to be at Fishbourne, situated at the mouth of Wootton Creek some two miles to the east of Ryde, where two acres of land on the west bank were purchased from Mr H.E. Dennis for a new terminal. A concrete slipway and approach road at right angles to the water were constructed and a channel dredged to give a minimum of 8 ft of water at low spring tides. Upstream from the slipway a large basin was also dredged to permit swinging and mooring of the tugs. The new terminal, costing a total of £17,730, comprised slipway, supervisor's residence, office, waiting rooms, car parking area, petrol pump and livestock pens, together with a new concrete road leading down to the slipway. The service opened on 15 March 1926, with a number of V.I.P.'s making the first crossing. Bert Butcher, employed on the ferry service for 45 years, and who retired in 1965, recorded his impressions of the day's proceedings thus:

"Before boarding the tow boat the party had watched the first cars being reversed down the slipway, with the driver controlling the brakes and a sailor standing on the running board looking after the steering. There was, of course, no cover aboard and, after setting off, a fresh wind whipped up the sea, sending sheets of spray sweeping over the party. By the time we got to Fishbourne they were very wet and miserable people, and decided to forego the pleasure of a return trip by barge in favour of the more conventional and drier passenger steamer from Ryde".

However, such was its success, in spite of the rigours of the 1¼ hour crossing, often with livestock as fellow passengers, that in the first twelve months operation more than 4,000 cars were carried. Each tow boat was capable of carrying up to five cars and at peak periods it was not unusual for three fully loaded boats to be hauled by a single tug. Motorists were given the option of travelling independently by passenger steamer while their car was being towed across, although this could be less convenient than remaining with their vehicle.

Plate 16. A rather poor shot taken from the 1861 pier, and showing cars being loaded onto a towboat at Lymington old slipway from the seaward end. (Bert Moody collection)

Plate 13. *Solent* at the Railway pier and *Carrier* with towboat heading downstream to Yarmouth. (The late A.M.S. Russell collection)

If the lot of the motorist using these services was thought to be disagreeable, what then of the tow boat crews? There were usually two men to each boat who worked for up to 16 hours per day. There was no shelter whatsoever on the boats, which had only 4ft freeboard, and in all but the calmest and most equable conditions sou'westers, oilskins and leather thigh boots were the crews standard garb, the latter also giving protection from the hooves of cattle. The state of the deck at the end of a crossing with a good load of livestock aboard can easily be imagined and a thorough sluicing down was necessary after virtually every passage, followed by pumping out by hand! Surprisingly, a number of the tow boat men lived to a ripe old age — food for thought in these days of centrally heated floating greenhouses.

With the Fishbourne slipway at right angles to the creek itself the tow boat had first to be brought alongside the tug, turned stern first to the jetty, released, and poled up onto the slipway. Because of the very short stern door substantial loading boards of stout timber, bound with iron and very heavy to handle, were necessary to permit easy embarkation of motor vehicles, which were backed on and driven off forwards at all terminals. Once unloading and reloading was completed the boat was poled out into the fairway and taken in tow by the waiting tug, and when one considers that sometimes three boats formed a single tow it is evident that a high degree of skill was essential. An article in the 1 June 1926 issue of the 'Motor' magazine headed "The Truth about the New Isle of Wight Service" described a visit to the island by car, using the Portsmouth-Fishbourne tow boat service, in the following words:

"We took the 2.00pm service on Saturday, May 22nd, and returned by the 3.30pm service on Monday, May 24th. On the outward journey the embarkation of the cars began at 1.30pm. There were 18 of them and three barges were required. Each car is reversed down the rather steep slipway with one the sailors standing on the running-board or walking beside the car holding the steering wheel, leaving the driver only to control the brakes. Two wooden runways connect the slipway with the barge. Only one car can be manoeurved at a time, at present. The total time taken in loading 18 cars was 40 minutes — a little over 2 minutes per car. Later on, it is intended to widen the slip-way so that two barges at once can be loaded, which will reduce the time. The start was delayed until 2.20 and, owing to it being low tide, a longer detour than usual had to be taken, so that the other side was not reached until after 3.30pm. The crossing was perfectly smooth and no covers for the cars were required or used. As the cars at the other end had only to be driven straight off the barges on to the slipway there was little time lost in disembarkation, but,

again, widening the slipway will save some minutes lost in getting the barges into position.

On the return journey the barges were manoeuvred into position at 3 o'clock, embarkation having already begun on a barge in position earlier, and the return journey started promptly at 3.30pm, reaching Portsmouth at 4.30pm, the cars being all off the slipway about 10 minutes later.

No Emptying of Tanks

Short of having a large ferry boat on to which the cars can be driven direct, the accomplishment of which, in view of the rise and fall of the tide, might prove to be difficult, we do not see that much time could be saved, whichever route is taken to cross to the Isle of Wight. One has to bear in mind that there are no formalities, no emptying of petrol tanks and replenishing, and that the cars are handled very skilfully indeed, without scratching a wing or causing any anxiety. The slipways are washed down after every tide and sanded so that they are not slippery, and we consider the embarkation and disembarkation perfectly safe. On the return journey a wave from a Union-Castle liner caused the tow-boats to rock slightly, but no water was shipped. At the same time this part of Spithead can be fairly rough, when bad sailors had, perhaps, better take the smoother passage from Lymington to Yarmouth, which is about half the distance. Against this is the fact that the journey from London (to Portsmouth, 70 miles) is increased to 94 miles, and it costs more to take the car across.

The passengers sit in their cars going across the water and the journey is not an uninteresting one, especially if one of the big liners is passed en route.

The week-day service is from Portsmouth at 10.00am and 2.00pm and from Fishbourne at 11.30am and 3.30pm, but at holiday times additional passages are run and also a Sunday service. A Sunday service may be run in the holiday months. The cars should be in readiness half an hour before the advertised time of starting, and notice should be given in advance at present."

However, the transfer of the service to Fishbourne was merely the first part of a co-ordinated plan to dispense with the tow boats (or horse boats as they were then known) and to replace them with vessels more in keeping with the modern image of the Southern Railway.

Plate 14. The original slipway at Broad Street, Portsmouth. Motorists in 1988 would put up their hands in horror of their vessels were to be taken to sea in such a way as this. In the twenties a trip in this fashion was all part of the adventure of motoring. (R. Butcher collection)

Plate 15. *Carrier* off Lymington with two towboats. She had a Passenger Certificate for 290. (Bert Moody collection)

Plate 16. Unloading cars at Fishbourne, with a tug lying off in Wooton Creek. Note the more sophisticated ramps in use here. (R. Butcher collection)

The First Car Ferries

Following the 1923 railway amalgamations the newly formed Southern Railway pursued a vigorous policy of improving and expanding its services to the Isle of Wight. Ryde pier was purchased in 1924 and three new passenger paddle steamers, *Shanklin*, *Merstone* and *Portsdown* were introduced between 1924 and 1928 on the Portsmouth-Ryde route whilst a similar but smaller vessel, the *Freshwater*, was added to the Lymington fleet in 1927. The marked increase in motor transport during the twenties and the potential growth of such traffic to the Isle of Wight consequent on improved facilities was principally responsible for the decision to replace the obsolescent tow-boat service as quickly as possible; indeed, even with the totally inadequate conditions prevailing the number of motor vehicles conveyed between Portsmouth and Ryde increased from 1168 in 1923 to 1356 in 1924 and in 1925 reached 1718, the last full year on this route. The transfer of the service from Ryde to Fishbourne effected a considerable advancement by eliminating tidal restrictions and was rewarded by traffic more than doubling to almost 4000 in 1926.

Mr Dashper, the Southern Railway Superintendent Mechanical (ie. Marine) Engineer, based at Southampton, was accordingly instructed by Gilbert Szlumper, the Docks & Marine Manager, to investigate the replacement of the horse boats by purpose-built self-propelled vessels which would meet the following conditions:-

1) Increased capacity
2) Easier and quicker loading
3) Reduced time on passage
4) Improved facilities for passengers
5) Greater economy

Needless to say, these conditions had to be met at minimum expenditure, and Mr Dashper seized the opportunity to informally discuss the matter with Sir Maurice Denny, chairman of the Dumbarton shipbuilding firm William Denny & Bros., during one of the latter's periodic visits to the Southern Railway. However, in spite of this Mr Dashper and his staff were unable to come up with any positive solution to the problem, and little progress was made during the next twelve months. The main stumbling block appeared to be the terminals, since Mr Dashper considered the existing slipways to be unsuitable for use by self-propelled ferries, partly on account of possible damage to the rudders and propellers, and deemed the use of pontoons to be essential. Bow loading at Portsmouth and side loading at Fishbourne was envisaged with the proposed vessel being fitted with a turntable to facilitate the compact stowage of vehicles. However, this scheme, apart from the expense, was bedevilled by the fact that the slipway at Portsmouth was public property and there was no other suitable space on the waterfront at that time where the Southern could construct their own private terminal. Correspondence between Mr Dashper and Sir Maurice reveals the former's perplexity and increasing desperation, and in

the end the problem was handed over to Sir Maurice. An outline specification for a vessel some 100 feet in length and having a service speed of 8 knots was drawn up and on 26 October 1926 a letter signed by Gilbert Szlumper was sent to Denny's asking them to submit a design for a self-propelled ferry to convey motor vehicles and livestock between Portsmouth and Fishbourne. The type of terminal to be used was left open. After some correspondence and discussion concerning slipway gradients and loading arrangements Denny's were of the opinion that they could design a vessel which would fulfil the owner's requirements and also be capable of using the existing slipways. Great was the joy of Mr Dashper — and Major Szlumper — on receiving this intelligence, since the General Manager was becoming a little restive at the apparent lack of progress. The design finally submitted by Denny's was for a double-ended, double twin screw, double twin rudder motor vessel with loading ramps at each end which would permit motor vehicles to drive-on, drive-off without the need for any reversing or manoeuvring and without having to swing the vessel whilst on passage. In other words, vehicles would embark over the stern and unload over the bow, the bow of the vessel on one crossing becoming the stern on the return. The design was put out to tender, and at their meeting on 26 January 1927 the Southern Railway Docks & Marine Committee recommended that in view of the increased traffic being conveyed between Portsmouth and Fishbourne as a result of opening the new route a self-propelled motor ferry boat be ordered from William Denny & Bros at a cost of £12,700.

The new vessel, christened *Fishbourne*, was launched on 21 June 1927, and the 'Lennox Herald' duly reported the event in the following words:

"The motor vessel *Fishbourne* was launched on Tuesday by William Denny & Bros. Ltd., Dumbarton, to the order of the Southern Railway Company for ferry service between Portsmouth and Fishbourne, (Isle of Wight). She is 131 feet long by 25 feet broad and 8 feet deep and will be able to carry about 16 motor cars, in addition to bicycles etc. The machinery consists of two Gardner crude oil engines each fitted with a propeller at each end of the vessel, all propellers being engaged or disengaged by means of clutches. The naming ceremony at the launch was performed by Mrs Dashper, wife of the superintending mechanical engineer of the owners' company.

The launching party then adjourned to the Luncheon Room of the yard, where success to the *Fishbourne* and her God-mother was duly pledged. Mr Denny, in the course of a short speech said it was ten months since a launch had taken place at the Leven Shipyard. He was safe in saying that it was a record — a melancholy record — due largely to the coal strike. Fortunately, things were now brighter, and with any luck at all there should be five launches within the next ten months. They had just seen launched a very interesting little ship. *Fishbourne* was odd in that it was double-ended and

Plate 17. Pioneer car ferry *Fishbourne* on the slip at Dumbarton prior to launching. Note the double twin screws and rudders mounted as so not to foul the slipways.
(Alan Brown collection)

Plate 18. *Fishbourne* in service. Note the manually operated ramps which were counterbalanced. The weights can be seen in the upper position as the vessel is on passage.
(R. Butcher collection)

Plate 19. Cars disembarking at Broad Street slipway, Portsmouth. Note the buildings on right, associated with the old Portsmouth-Gosport vehicle ferry — what a boon this would be today.
(R. Butcher collection)

Plate 20. A damaged shot, but the collection of vintage cars would make an enthusiast very excited today. The original double ended concept of these vessels was not successful, and *Fishbourne* ran bow first on every crossing, maneuvering as necessary at the terminals to permit drive through operation.
(R. Butcher collection)

had four-times of everything, except perhaps the captain — four rudders, four screws and so on. He hoped she would make so much money for her owners that a second boat would be necessary. It was a pleasure for many reasons for his firm to build ships for the Southern Railway and one person he would like to mention was their superintendent, Mr Dashper. It was always a pleasure to be supervised by a gentleman who knew his business, and from first to last, from truck to keel, there is no part on any ship they supplied to the Southern Railway about which they could not ask advice from Mr Dashper and receive a definite and proper reply."

Sir Maurice must have been a kindly man!

Although Sir Maurice omitted to mention it, *Fishbourne* was at the time the largest vessel of her type to be built for service in Great Britain. Her capacity was, in fact, slightly greater than that stated by Sir Maurice, since it was calculated that the maximum load would be 17-18 average sized cars. The main deck was completely clear of obstructions and had large retractable loading ramps at each end which eliminated the previous necessity of having to use loading boards. The propellers and rudders were set well back to preclude any danger of damage when running onto the slipways, and clutches were provided to enable the bow propellers to run idle whilst on passage, these being used purely for manoeuvring purposes. Foot passengers were not carried, but accommodation to meet Board of Trade requirements for motor vehicle occupants was provided and consisted of toilets in the deck houses beneath the bridge and rather sparsely furnished separate saloons for Ladies and Gentlemen, whilst after the spartan conditions on the tow boats the provision of a wheelhouse and other shelter for the crew was the height of luxury. The increased draft of the new ship necessitated extra dredging at Fishbourne, together with the provision of dolphins to assist in berthing, whilst at Portsmouth an oil fuel storage tank was provided.

Fishbourne's entry into service was, surprisingly, a very low key affair and received only the briefest mention in the local press; whether teething troubles were anticipated on account of the novel design of the vessel is not clear, but the precaution was certainly a wise one. She made a trial trip between Southampton and Fishbourne on Wednesday 13 July and entered service between Portsmouth and Fishbourne on the 23rd, making two return crossings daily at an average passage time of 55 minutes. At the end of each crossing the connections from the ships' wheel had to be changed over from one set of rudders to the other, but unfortunately the mechanical arrangements intended to enable this to be effected proved unsatisfactory and *Fishbourne* had to be withdrawn and the tow boats reinstated while the problem was investigated. As no practical solution could be found she returned to service and thereafter operated as a conventional ship, sailing bow first on every crossing. Since she was a true double ended vessel, but not entirely symmetrical, the bow was identified by the position of the stump mast (at the forward end of the wheelhouse) and by the extension of the deck houses, which protruded forward of the bridge. Under the new arrangements *Fishbourne* berthed bow-on at the island terminal and after loading backed off the slipway, canted her stern into the basin and headed bow first out of the creek. On arrival at Portsmouth a rope was dropped from the bow into a waiting boat and made fast to a buoy situated in the entrance to the Camber while *Fishbourne* backed stern first up to the slipway, where the stern lines were secured to an old cannon embedded into the beach. The ramps were manually operated — a slow and laborious task requiring the services of four men — and two pillar like structures adjacent to each ramp housed the necessary gear, which was eventually replaced by electrically operated winches. The bow rudders were also removed after bow-first operation on all runs had become the norm. Occasionally, under adverse conditions, the motor boat *Alice* would assist by holding *Fishbourne* against wind or tide whilst she manoeuvred onto the slip-way. *Alice*, incidentally, was purchased in 1928 to succeed the last of the steam tugs, *Adur II*, which was then sold to the Shoreham Harbour Trust.

Fishbourne was joined by a slightly larger and improved sister ship, the *Wootton*, delivered from Dumbarton at Southampton on Thursday 21 June 1928, and with typical Southern panache a massive publicity campaign was initiated to coincide with her entry into service. Posters showing pictures of motor cars embarking at Portsmouth and disembarking on the island, and exhorting motorists to 'drive on, drive off the new ferries', were distributed on railway stations and elsewhere over the whole country, and once again a huge surge of traffic to the island followed this further improvement in the service. *Wootton* differed slightly in detail from her elder sister, a single more comfortably furnished saloon, complete with refreshment facilities, replaced the latter's separate saloons, whilst the bridge and deck houses presented a rather different profile. An anchor was provided at the bow only, and the bow rudders were omitted.

On completion of the 1929 season the General Manager reported that the increase in traffic warranted a further vessel and recommended that an order be placed with William Denny & Bros., for its construction at an estimated cost of approximately £17,500. The new vessel, named *Hilsea* and delivered at Southampton on 14 June 1930, was vitually a repeat of *Wootton*, though reputedly half a knot faster. Traffic continued to increase by leaps and bounds, and during summer week-ends the three ships were hard pressed to cope, making no fewer than 15 round trips between them on Saturdays. The courage and enterprise of the Southern Railway in modernising its services to the island was certainly paying dividends and even though heavy traffic was largely seasonal the improved facilities encouraged additional travel, both passenger and vehicle, during the remainder of the year. During the war years only one vessel was used on the public service, the other two being occupied on military duties. Both *Fishbourne* and *Wootton* were involved in the Dunkirk evacuation, and although they reached the French shore they were not actually used to transport troops back to Britain. The Southern Railway thus had every reason to be grateful to Denny's, whose expertise and skills had enabled them to provide a simple, convenient and economic replacement for the tow boats, and laid the foundation for a service between Portsmouth and Fishbourne which has remained, with periodical improvements and up-dating, as the major vehicle ferry route to the island.

The Southampton company had also modernised, if that is the correct word, their own motor vehicle transport service, and their method makes an interesting contrast to that adopted by the Southern. The passenger steamers had space on the foredeck for only a very limited number of cars but during the 1927/28 winter the 42-year-old paddle steamer *Her Majesty* was converted into a car carrier, although still retaining some passenger accommodation. The for'd companionway was removed, the foremast set as far back as possible and the after deck saloon completely cut away in order to leave large open deck spaces fore and aft of the machinery, capable of accommodating a total of around 18 cars. These were side loaded from the pontoons and when necessary cars were swung round through 90° on the deck by means of 'skids' placed under the rear wheels. The system worked well and the chief officer and bosun became very skilled in eying up the cars and selecting each one for a certain position in order to utilise the available space to the greatest advantage. The first car in the queue allocated to that sailing was not necessarily the first to be embarked, much to the consternation of the driver of the vehicle occupying that favoured position! Really heavy traffic (for those days) was however concentrated into a few peak summer Saturdays, plus the Easter and Whitsuntide holidays week-ends, and *Her Majesty* generally appeared in service only during these peaks, or when on tendering or relief duties. During the 'thirties the cargo steamer *Lord Elgin* was also pressed into service on peak summer Saturday afternoons and made one, or two if necessary, return trips to Cowes carrying cars only. Usually, the ships on the normal packet service were well able to cope with any vehicular traffic and the conversion of *Her Majesty* can perhaps be best regarded as a response, at minimum capital expenditure, to the threat posed by the new Southern Railway car ferries. Red Funnel policy, in general, has been to carry passengers and cars on the same ship and the isolated conversion of *Her Majesty* was followed by the building of *Medina*, (1931), *Gracie Fields* (1936) and *Vecta* (1938) — vessels which carried on the traditional service but having greater capacity and comfort than the ships they replaced. Since the demise of *Lord Elgin* Red Funnel have not only carried passengers and cars on each ship but also freight (now by lorries, wheeled trailers, etc.) and coaches, although of course the hydrofoils do provide a complementary passenger only service.

Meanwhile, at Lymington, the tow boats soldiered on until 1938.

Plate 21. (Above). *Her Majesty* backing out of Cowes. She was converted to a car carrier in 1927/28, but also was used to tender to the liners. (the late Fred A. Plant)

Plate 22. *Princess Elizabeth* approaching the pontoon at Royal Pier, Southampton. The Southampton Co., retained the open foredeck design of paddle steamer for the very purpose of car carrying. (Red Funnel)

Plate 23. *Princess Elizabeth* loading cars from the Royal Pier pontoon, Southampton. The crews became very skilled in packing in as many cars as possible on any one crossing. (Red Funnel)

Plate 24. (Below), *Princess Elizabeth* approaching Cowes. The pontoon is on the right and two crew members stand on the sponsons ready to put lines ashore. (Gavin Johnston collection)

Developments at Lymington

Since the arrival of the railway at Lymington improving the means of communication between the mainland and western Wight, other than by developments in the steamer service, had centred on the provision of a railway tunnel under the Solent. This scheme had been originally mooted circa 1885, but the first practical steps were not taken until 1901, when the South Western & Isle of Wight Junction Railway was formed with the object of linking the London & South Western and Freshwater Yarmouth & Newport railways. The proposed line was to have diverged from the Lymington branch at a point some 1¼ miles north of Lymington Town Station, run almost four miles due south to Keyhaven Marshes, where it would have crossed to the Island via a 2½ mile single track tunnel beneath the western Solent and then emerged just to the west of the River Yar midway between Yarmouth and Freshwater. Here the line would have divided and crossed the river on two separate bridges joining the Freshwater, Yarmouth & Newport metals in both a northbound and southbound direction. Although some test bores were made in the vicinity of Totland the scheme lapsed but was revived in 1920 when a deputation from the Island endeavoured to obtain financial

support from the Government. In the then current financial climate the proposal met with scant enthusiasm, but it was not until 1927 that the Ministry of Transport finally informed the County Council the anticipated increase in traffic would be insufficient to justify the large capital expenditure required and the scheme was abandoned.

The success of the new self-propelled vehicle ferries on the Fishbourne service, in terms of increased traffic, encouraged the Southern Railway in 1927 to consider the introduction of similar vessels on the Yarmouth route, particularly since a record 1269 vehicles had been carried by the tow boats in 1925/26. However, the existing terminal facilities at both Lymington and Yarmouth were quite inadequate for the proposed vessels, and one of the first steps taken by the railway company was to write to the Yarmouth Town Trust, outlining their plans and enquiring whether suitable facilities could be provided in the harbour. These proposals were received enthusiastically by the Yarmouth authorities, who offered to enlarge the existing slipway, subject to the necessary dredging being carried

Plate 25. *Jumsey* at Yarmouth. Note the petrol tanker in the towboat, which is being swung stern first for unloading at the slipway. (isle of Wight Steam Railway collection)

Plate 26. (Below), Unloading at Yarmouth, the tow boat having been successfully maneouvered stern first onto the slipway. Note the new work on the pier face in readiness of things to come! (Isle of Wight Steam Railway collection)

Plate 27. Aerial view of Lymington pier in pre-car ferry days. (B. Wales)

Plate 28. (Below). The pier station and pier from upriver, looking to seaward. Motor train at the platform. (late AMS Russell collection)

out by the Southern Railway.

While these negotiations were in progress a west Wight business man, Mr Frank Aman of Totland, who had been a prominent promoter and supporter of the Solent Tunnel scheme, wrote to Sir Herbert Walker, the General Manager of the Southern Railway, explaining his own plans for introducing a privately owned vehicle ferry service across the Solent between Keyhaven and Sconce Point and seeking financial support from the railway company for his proposed venture. On 23 July 1931 the General Manager reported to the Southern Railway Board details of the correspondence which had passed between Mr Aman and himself on the subject of the proposed ferry and after discussion it was decided that the company could take no financial interest in the scheme. This did not mean that the railway company was disinterested in the proposals however — far from it — as it was further decided that their own plans for improving the Lymington-Yarmouth service be held in abeyance. In spite of this financial set-back Mr Aman must have felt sufficiently encouraged to proceed further with his scheme.

Meanwhile, news of the proposed new ferry service between Keyhaven and Sconce Point had appeared in the local press and this, coupled with the silence of Southern Railway on the subject of its own proposals prompted the Yarmouth Harbour Commissioners to enquire whether or not the railway company had any interest in the new ferry. The answer was to the effect that the Southern Railway had considered this scheme, but had turned it down on the grounds of expense. This evasive reply by no means satisfied the Commissioners, and a further enquiry at the end of 1931 elicited the following somewhat ominous reponse from Mr G.R. Newcombe, the Southern Railway Docks & Marine manager at Southampton:

"We still have the whole question under consideration, but, in view of the serious financial situation, we are endeavouring to ascertain if there are any ways and means by which the somewhat heavy expense involved in introducing the new service can be curtailed".

It was, at least, a slightly more honest reply!

A full three years passed before the subject of the Keyhaven ferry was again raised at Board level, when the General Manager, at the October 1934 meeting, disclosed that detailed particulars had been received from Mr Aman and that copies of these had been circulated amongst the directors. After some discussion the General Manager

was instructed to explore the matter further and report back to the Board in due course. Sir Herbert Walker proved to be a very quick worker, and as a result of the Southern Railway's covert dealings with Mr Aman he was able to submit the Heads of a Proposed Agreement between the Company and Mr J.H. Cogswell (as Trustee on behalf of the proposed Ferry Company) at the next Board meeting, held on 22 November. The Agreement provided, inter alia:

1) That subject to the ferry service being completed and brought into use not later than the 30th June 1936, the Railway Company will abandon its present service between Lymington and the Isle of Wight and transfer to the Ferry Company the property now belonging to this Company from the bridge over the Lymington River (with access thereto) on the southern side of Lymington Town Station to and including the Pier Station as well as the two passenger steamers, four cargo boats and one motor launch at present engaged in the service.

2) That a sum of approx £63,500, subject to adjustment according to the day of payment, will be paid by the Ferry Company as compensation for loss of traffic and consideration for the transfer of the assets mentioned in Clause (1).

3) That the said sum will be paid to the Railway Company within 3 months of the date of the opening of the ferry service.

4) That the Railway Company and the Ferry Company will work together to carry on the Ferry Company's undertaking to their mutual advantage.

Some ten months later, on 10 October 1935, the General Manager again reported to the Board that although he had informed Mr Aman that Parliamentary authority would be necessary before he could proceed with his scheme for a ferry service between Keyhaven and the Isle of Wight, he had failed to get a satisfactory assurance from Mr Aman that he would endeavour to obtain that Authority or proceed

Plate 29. *Bebington,* built in 1925, on the Mersey. Designed purely for the carriage of vehicles these vessels were made redundant by the opening of the Mersey Tunnel. Loading was from pontoons via ramps fitted to the ships, which were also double ended with twin screws and a single rudder at each end. (J. Clarkson)

Plate 30. *Barnston* on passage. She finally went to Dutch owners in 1939/40. (J. Clarkson)

without it. The General Manager explained the position with regard to the Company's present service between Lymington and Yarmouth and outlined certain improvements which would be necessary if that service was to be continued. He recommended that Mr Aman be informed of the Company's intention to include in their Bill of next Session the necessary powers to enable effect to be given to their proposals at Lymington on the understanding that if Mr Aman should decide to proceed with his scheme and obtain the necessary authority in the next session of Parliament the company would be ready to associate with him in carrying it out; provided an Agreement satisfactory to the Company could be reached and sanctioned by Parliament and that Mr Aman, or the Company he may be forming for the purpose, was able to raise the necessary money to carry it out, including the money required to meet any sum agreed to be paid to the Company. Further, that if the necessary powers for the scheme were not obtained, or an Agreement satisfactory to the Company could not be reached or given effect to, the Company to be free to proceed with their own proposals (to improve Lymington to Yarmouth services).

By 30th January 1936 an agreement between the Isle of Wight Ferry, Mr Aman and the Southern Railway Company had been reached and sealed, as follows:

"The Agreement provides that in the event of a Provisional Order for which the Ferry Company had applied being made and confirmed by Parliament the parties will enter into an Agreement in the form as scheduled to the present Agreement and that in consideration of the execution of the present Agreement the Company will refrain from opposing the Provisional Order.

The scheduled form of Agreement provides (inter alia) that the Ferry Company will, within six months of the passing of the Act confirming the Provisional Order raise the capital required for the construction of the necessary works and the provision of at least two ferry boats as well as for the payment to this Company of the sum of £61,592 as compensation for the loss of traffic and consideration of the transfer of the assets mentioned in Clause (1) of the minute of the 22nd November 1934.

Subject to compliance with this condition the Company will not proceed with the contemplated improvements at Lymington Pier Station, for which powers are being sought in the Bill at present before Parliament, and will withdraw the service between Lymington and Yarmouth when the new ferry service is running.

In the event of the Ferry Company being unable to raise the Capital required, the Powers of the Order are not to be exercised or transferred by them, no ferry is to be instituted by them, and the Railway Company is to be at liberty to proceed with the improvement of its own service."

In order to cover themselves whatever the outcome of Mr Aman's proposals, the Southern Railway sought Powers during the 1935/36 session of Parliament which would enable them:

1) To acquire tidal lands for the purpose of a quay and slipway adjacent to Lymington Pier Station, which had been agreed by the Lymington Town Council subject to any necessary dredging of the river being effected by the company.

2) To discontinue their steamer service between Lymington and Yarmouth and to transfer to the Isle of Wight Ferry Company the vessels employed on this service together with the property at Lymington Pier Station.

Great consideration was caused at Yarmouth when details of the Bill and its contradictory clauses became known, since two-thirds of the harbour revenue accrued from the Lymington service and some £15,500 had been expended by the Harbour Commissioners or their predecessors in the provision of facilities for the railway passenger and goods vessels. Negotiations between the railway company and the Harbour Commissioners concerning the proposed modernised car ferry service had also continued — albeit inconclusively — until mid-1935, when these were abruptly broken off by the former when they were about to deposit their Bill in Parliament. Both Yarmouth and the Isle of Wight County Council opposed the Bill, and it was not until they had received certain assurances from the railway company that they agreed to withdraw their opposition. What these assurances were is not clear but it is probable that the railway company already felt reasonably certain — as did most other parties — that the Isle of Wight Ferry Company could not raise sufficient

capital to enable it to proceed with the scheme. Nevertheless Yarmouth continued to be anxious about the future of the Lymington service and a further enquiry to the railway company in January 1937 brought the usual response expressing regret at not yet being able to give any definite information. By this time, however, it had become perfectly clear to the Southern Railway that the Ferry Company was in great financial difficulty, and quite unable to commence the service before the agreed time limit expired on 31 December 1937. The railway company therefore resolved to go ahead with their own scheme, and in February 1937 the General manager wrote to the Yarmouth Harbour Commissioners informing them of the company's decision to proceed with their plans for modernising the Lymington service, which included the construction of a new slipway and other works at Lymington Pier Station and the building of a new steamer having sufficient passenger accommodation to operate the winter passenger service as well as carry motor vehicles and goods. During the first week of March a meeting between railway officials and the Harbour Commissioners to discuss the arrangements for improving the facilities at Yarmouth Quay took place and resulted in the Commissioners agreeing to purchase a range of old buildings fronting the quay for conversion into waiting rooms and offices, together with the construction of an enlarged slipway and the necessary dredging.

In spite of the failure of the Keyhaven project to materialise it is not without interest to review the steps actually taken by Mr Aman with regard to the proposed terminals and the ships, together with the manner in which the service was intended to be operated. With the refusal of financial support from the railway company the scheme was doomed from the outset, but Mr Aman may well have misinterpreted the company's interest and actions as a sign that financial assistance would possibly be forthcoming in the case of need. Certainly he must have felt sufficiently encouraged to proceed, and in the hope of being able to raise sufficient capital to complete his scheme the optimistic Mr Aman bought a disused pier near Yarmouth, had plans prepared for a pier at Keyhaven, negotiated for the purchase of two ferry vessels and applied to Parliament for powers to operate the service. The scheme was not without its advantages, especially with regard to the transport of motor vehicles, but the needs of local foot passengers and rail travellers were probably better served by the Lymington-Yarmouth service. Surprisingly, Lymington Town Council appeared to be in favour of the Keyhaven route, for reasons not altogether connected with the transport needs of the local inhabitants, since one official, rubbing his hands, incautiously remarked that the development of the Keyhaven Estate would result in rateable values being considerably increased!

The disused pier, purchased from the War Department in 1933, was situated at Fort Victoria, Sconce Point, about one mile west of Yarmouth and to render this suitable for use by side loading ferries it was proposed to extend the pier head by 50ft at each side, although it is not clear how it was intended to cope with tidal variations. On the mainland, it was proposed to construct an embankment extending for 3,300 feet over the foreshore from a point on the high water mark of ordinary tides about 600 yards eastwards of Keyhaven, and a pier some 1000 feet in length of open concrete construction, in continuation of the embankment. A road was to be built on top of the embankment and then continued landwards to link up with the main road between Lymington and Bournemouth in the vicinity of Pennington. Once again, no indication of how tidal variations were to be coped with was given.

As for the vessels themselves a provisional agreement had been reached in June 1935 between the Isle of Wight Ferry Company and Birkenhead Corporation for the purchase of the goods ferry boats *Bebington* and *Oxton*. These two vessels had previously been used for the transport of vehicles and goods across the Mersey between Birkenhead and Liverpool, and had been rendered redundant by the opening of the Mersey Road Tunnel. Built in 1925, and of 732 gross tons, they were 143 feet in length and exceptionally broad beamed at 50 ft. Machinery consisted of two sets of three cylinder triple expansion reciprocating steam engines, each coupled to screws fore and aft, thus making them of the so called double twin screw arrangement. No passenger accommodation was provided since this traffic was separately catered for by passenger ferries. Some reservations concerning the suitability of such vessels for use in the exposed waters of the western Solent were expressed even though the Mersey itself could be surprisingly boisterous at times.

It was anticipated that *Bebington* and *Oxton* would be able to make the crossing between Keyhaven and Fort Victoria in ten minutes; surely a rather optimistic assessment requiring an average speed of 8 knots. Passengers travelling by rail would alight at Brockenhurst, where buses would convey them to the Island without further change of vehicle, since the buses themselves would be transported across the Solent on the ferries and then continue to various Island destinations. Presumably it was also intended for local foot passengers to be picked up and conveyed to the Island in buses.

As time passed it became increasingly obvious that the Ferry Company was experiencing serious financial problems, and on 17 June 1935 the Birkenhead Town Clerk reported that the option to purchase the two ferries had been extended to 30 June 1936 at the request of the company. Further requests for an extension were subsequently made but by March 1937 the Corporation, exasperated by the Ferry Company's procrastination, stipulated that payment had to be made by 31 May of that year. The seriousness of the company's financial plight was further exposed, in response to the deadline, by requesting an option to purchase two older goods ferry steamers, the *Churton* and *Barnston*, in place of the *Bebington* and *Oxton*. After discussions with representatives of the company the Corporation agreed to accept the offer of the company to purchase the *Churton* and *Barnston* at a price of £8000 each on or before 30 September 1937, subject to a deposit of £2000 by the company and the payment of actual out-of-pocket expenses for maintenance, dock dues etc., until completion. Both vessels were of similar size to *Bebington* and *Oxton*, but four years older. Once again requests for extensions were made, and in June 1938 the Town Clerk reported that arrears for the maintenance of the steamers at the date of the expiration of the company's option to purchase, namely

31 December 1937, amounted to £449 5s 4d. The vessels were advertised for sale and on 18 May the Town Clerk reported to the Council on the financial position of the Ferry Company. After discussion it was resolved:

"That no further proceedings be taken and that the amount owing be written off as irrecoverable".

Frank Aman died in 1939, aged 81 years, and thus came to an end the unhappy saga of the Keyhaven-Fort Victoria ferry service. The Southern Railway's role in the affair hardly appears to have been an honourable one, and in retrospect it is difficult to understand why persons of the acumen, integrity and standing of Sir Herbert Walker adopted such a course. The episode has been dealt with in considerable detail, since it had the effect of delaying the introduction of a modernised ferry service between Lymington and Yarmouth by some five or six years, and resulted in a completely different vessel being built from the ones originally envisaged. Without the dreams of Mr Aman *Lymington* would never have been built — or, at least, not in the revolutionary form in which she finally appeared in 1938.

Plate 31. Fishbourne slipway at low tide with *Hilsea* loading for the return trip to Portsmouth. The later ships had electric winches to operate the ramps, and improved passenger facilities.
(R. Butcher collection)

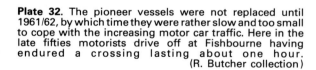

Plate 32. The pioneer vessels were not replaced until 1961/62, by which time they were rather slow and too small to cope with the increasing motor car traffic. Here in the late fifties motorists drive off at Fishbourne having endured a crossing lasting about one hour.
(R. Butcher collection)

Plate 33. The tow boats on the Lymington service became redundant in 1939, and can still be seen at Lymington at the spot where they were left and forgotten.
(Alan Brown collection)

CHAPTER 2

THE VOITH SCHNEIDER PROPELLER

Early Development

Prior to 1929 only two methods had been successfully employed for the propulsion of mechanically powered ships, namely the paddle wheel and screw propeller, although other ideas have been tried. Apart from some investigations involving pumps and jets, experiments had also been carried out with vertical bladed propellers, the first of these being in 1840 when a Norwegian captain took out a patent for the propulsion of a vessel by means of rotating vertical blades which, whilst theoretically feasible, proved impossible to transform into practice. Later, attempts to employ what was in effect a vertical stern paddle wheel with feathering floats were tried but, as can be imagined, the results proved markedly inferior to those obtained by conventional methods. Finally, around 1919, a patented vertical bladed propeller (the Kirsten Boeing) was fitted experimentally to two small American vessels, but manoeuvring problems made the method unacceptable and it was abandoned. It thus appeared that all attempts to usurp the paddle wheel or screw with a vertical bladed propeller were doomed to failure. It is perhaps difficult to envisage how a propulsive thrust could be obtained from a set of rotating vertical blades, let alone show any advantages over a paddle wheel or screw propeller, but it should be remembered that, in addition to rowing, a small boat could also be propelled by sculling. This technique, known to the ancient Chinese and based on the tail fin action of a fish (fig 1), produces both propulsive and steering forces by means of a single stern oar. It was this sculling action which inventors were trying to reproduce by mechanical means, but as it involved an oscillating motion superimposed on shallow figure of eight transverse sweeps it is not surprising that it had so far defied all attempts at successful mechanical reproduction.

However, what eventually proved to be a practical solution originated in a device conceived and developed for a purpose having no connection whatsoever with the propulsion of ships and which, in the event, proved to be unsuitable for its intended application due to the development of superior alternative methods. During the nineteen-twenties, far from the sea in central Europe, a Viennese engineer named Ernst Schneider conceived the idea of harnessing the power of broad, free-flowing rivers to generate electricity at low cost by the use of a new type of water turbine. This turbine consisted of a number of vertical blades rotating about a (vertical) axis but with each blade having a variable oscillating movement about its own axis superimposed on the general rotary motion of the blades. A simple and easily made adjustment to the eccentric controlling the blade oscillations permitted the maximum power to be absorbed by the turbine, whatever the direction of the current at that point, without the need to bodily turn the whole unit, and Schneider envisaged a number of turbine driven generators strung across a river with each turbine individually adjusted as necessary to produce its maximum output. Schneider had already constructed a miniature model of the turbine and during his holidays had tested its operation, with promising results, by immersing it into small streams and brooks. Whilst returning home on the Vienna express he made the acquaintance of Ludwig Kober, an employee of Messrs J.M. Voith, specialists in the development and manufacture of water turbines, pumps and other precision machinery, and the two men, discovering a mutual interest fell into conversation. Schneider showed the model turbine to his new friend, explained its purpose and then demonstrated its action by holding it out of the carriage window, whereupon it commenced to spin merrily round the breeze. Kober was impressed, so much so that he mentioned his meeting with Schneider to Herr Walter Voith, the director in charge of the company's St Polten works near Vienna, and as a result Schneider received an invitation to discuss his scheme with Herr Voith. At first, Voith, usually quite responsive to novel ideas was somewhat sceptical but eventually agreed to have tests carried out at the company's main works at Heidenheim, Germany, which proved his doubts to have been well founded, since the results indicated that the turbine would be impractical for use in its envisaged application. In addition, and perhaps more important, the variable pitch Kaplan turbine being developed at the same time showed a greater efficiency and a potentially higher maximum output than the Schneider design and was therefore a more attractive proposition. As a matter of interest, the cross-section of a modern run-of-river hydro-electric power station with Kaplan turbine is illustrated in fig 2. However, the Voith engineers were nothing if not thorough, and by reversing the process and driving the turbine as a pump it was found possible to obtain a thrust in any desired horizontal direction, solely by adjustment of the blade oscillatory control and without having to turn the unit in azimuth. It was quickly appreciated that this device successfully eliminated all the problems which had bedevilled previous attempts to design a practical vertical bladed propeller, and as such offered tremendous potential as a combined propulsion and steering unit for ships. This exciting discovery quickly led to further investigations being carried out at the Vienna Technical High School, using the circulating water channel of the Ship Technical Research Institute, and these showed such promising results that Voith decided to develop Schneider's invention purely as a ship propulsion unit. Thus was born the Voith-Schneider propeller.

Development work was carried out by a dedicated team of engineers in the newly formed Voith Schneider department at the St Polten Works and by 1928 the first propeller had been installed in a 60hp Maybach petrol engined motor launch ordered by Voith from the Lurssen shipyard, Bremen-Vegesack, for test and experimental purposes. This vessel appropriately christened Torqueo "I turn round" — underwent exhaustive trials on Lake Constance, astounding all concerned with its handling, manoeuvrability and reliability and encouraging Voith to go ahead and market the propeller. The first commercial vessel to utilise the new propulsion system was a tow boat named Uhu, built in 1931 for the Bayrisher Lloyd Company of Regensburg for service on the River Danube. To provide the necessary power and give greater manoeurability the Uhu was equipped with two stern mounted propellers driven by a pair of 350hp diesel engines, a layout which also permitted a small transverse thrust to be obtained.

The impressive performance of Torqueo on Lake Constance had not gone unnoticed by officials of the Deutsche Reichsbahn Gesellschaft (German State Railways), the owners and operators of a large fleet of passenger ships and ferries on the lake, who had embarked upon a comprehensive modernisation programme in the mid-nineteen twenties and had already replaced a number of ageing paddle steamers with new twin screw motor vessels. The advantages of Voith Schneider propulsion rendered it particularly suitable for the conditions experienced on the lake, and following the successful trials of Torqueo it was decided to try the Voith Schneider system on their next batch of new vessels. Accordingly, the three 1931 ships (Augsburg, Kempsten and Ravensburg) were all fitted with twin Voith Schneider units and proved so successful that Voith Schneider propulsion was thereafter standardised for all subsequent vessels, including those of the associated Austrian Federal Railway fleet. This was a major breakthrough for Voith, since there were now a number of VSP ships in a major fleet which could demonstrate, under actual service conditions, the advantages of this method of propulsion. In addition, the valuable operational experience gained led to propeller detail modifications and improvements, thereby enhancing their reliability and extending the service life between overhauls. By the outbreak of war in 1939 some 78 vessels world-wide had been fitted with Voith Schneider propellers, including passenger ships, car and train ferries, tugs, floating cranes, mine-sweepers and fire-floats — vessels which all required exceptional manoeuvring capabilities, predicable handling and precise positioning.

"There may be something in this Voith Schneider Business"

Although the introduction and application of the Voith Schneider propeller had not gone unreported in British shipping journals the fact that it was neither advertised nor marketed in this country during the early years resulted in little interest being aroused. Similarly, since previous vertical bladed propellers had proved markedly unsuccessful, British shipowners were understandably sceptical of the advantages claimed by this latest contender and it was not until 1934 that any positive moves were made to investigate its potential

19

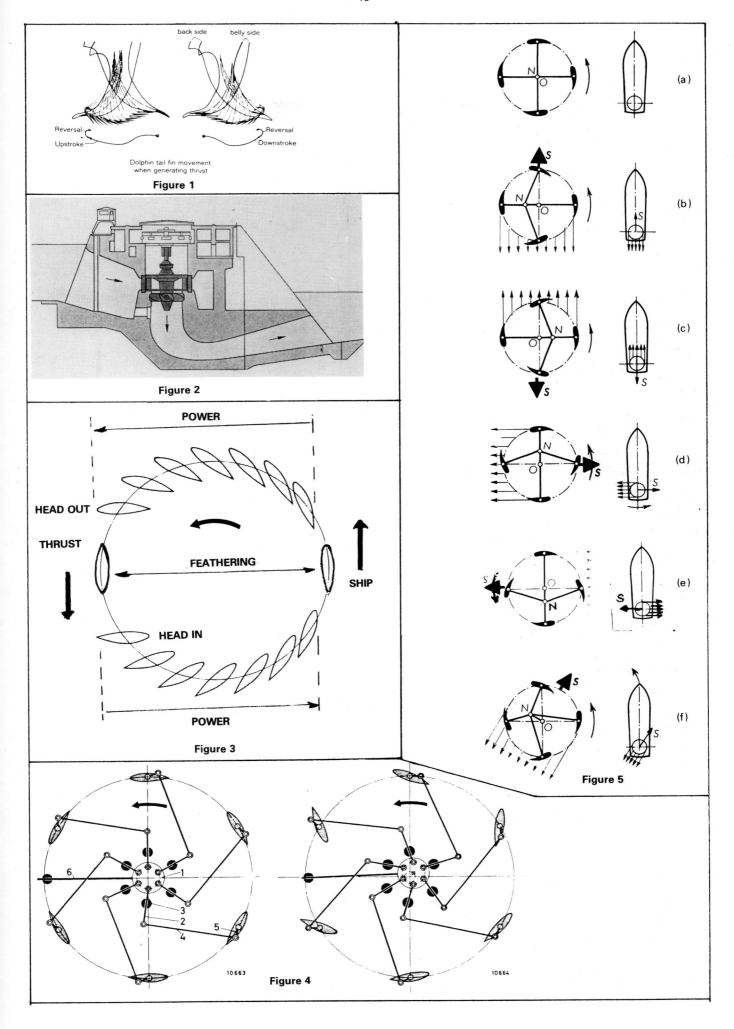

back side   belly side

Reversal
Upstroke

Reversal
Downstroke

Dolphin tail fin movement
when generating thrust

Figure 1

Figure 2

POWER

HEAD OUT

THRUST

FEATHERING

SHIP

HEAD IN

POWER

Figure 3

(a)

(b)

(c)

(d)

(e)

(f)

Figure 5

6

1

3
2
5
4

10663

10664

Figure 4

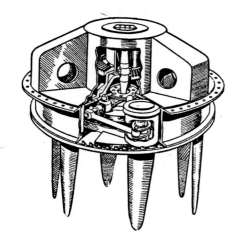

Figure 6

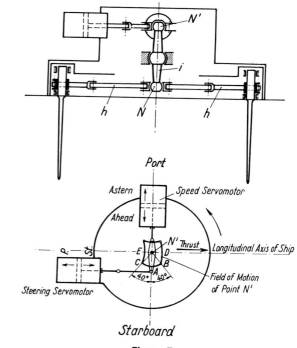

Figure 7

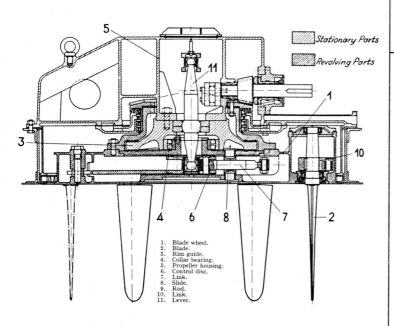

1. Blade wheel.
2. Blade.
3. Rim guide.
4. Collar bearing.
5. Propeller housing.
6. Control disc.
7. Link.
8. Slide.
9. Rod.
10. Link.
11. Lever.

Stationary Parts
Revolving Parts

Figure 8

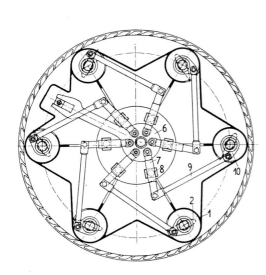

Figure 9

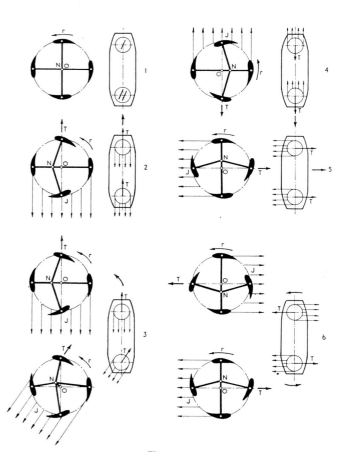

Figure 10

for British and Commonwealth applications. In that year a British naval architect, A.C. Hardy, crossed Lake Constance on one of the new Voith Schneider propelled motor ships which by chance happened to be on that particular crossing rather than a paddle steamer or normal twin screw vessel. Although Hardy was principal partner in the London based marine advisory and consultancy firm of Hardy, Tobin & Co., he was better known as a most prolific author of books and articles on maritime subjects. It was while returning via Lake Constance from a business trip to Zurich with Charles Birchall, proprietor of the Liverpool 'Journal of Commerce' that his attention was attracted by the extraordinary manoeuvrability of the ship on which they were travelling. The reason for this was quickly ascertained, and as a marine consultant his professional interest was at once aroused. He foresaw that Voith Schneider propulsion could be of advantage to British shipowners and operators, and with this in mind considered that its promotion in this country could be beneficial both to Voith and his own company. The partners in the consultancy were Hardy himself, T.V. Tobin, and Captain E.C. Goldsworthy, who had joined forces with Hardy and Tobin only the previous year. The three, naval architect, engineer and master mariner respectively were fully qualified to discuss and advise on any matters relating to a ship, its construction, propulsion or operation, and on his return to the office Hardy commented that "there may be something in this Voith Schneider business" and that it warranted "looking into". The first step was obviously to establish contact with Voith, and as Captain Goldsworthy was shortly to take a holiday at Lake Titisee in the Black Forest, arrangements were made for him to visit Voith, at their Heidenheim works, while in Germany.

J.M. Voith was a family concern whose main products were papermaking machinery and water turbines but they had also, as explained in the previous section, taken up the Schneider patent to develop and manufacture the Voith Schneider propeller. At the time of Captain Goldsworthy's visit, the firm was controlled by three brothers, Dr Hanns Voith, Dr Hermann Voith and Dr Walter Voith, whose grandfather had established the firm in the mid-nineteenth century, and which had expanded to become the major industry of the town. Captain Goldsworthy was received graciously, shown round the works by Herr Clerc, the chief engineer in charge of the Voith Schneider department, and finally introduced to Dr Hanns Voith. During the discussions Captain Goldsworthy made it known that his visit was not merely adademic, but with a view to Hardy, Tobin & Co., being of assistance to them in marketing the propeller in Great Britain, and with this end in view he expressed the desire to visit, examine and if possible handle a Voith Schneider ship. No sooner said than done — the telephone was picked up and arrangements made for him to join one of the German State Railway ships at Lindau on the following day, when every opportunity would be afforded to fulfil his request. The ninety mile journey from Heidenheim to Lake Constance was speedily covered next morning in a large Mercedes touring car, an exhilarating overture to the eagerly anticipated main activities of the day. At Lindau the party boarded the MV Augsburg, a 148ft diesel engined passenger ship built in 1931 with direct drive to the twin Voith Schneider units at the stern. After being welcomed by the captain the party was shown over the vessel and were at once impressed by its spotless condition, the neat appearance and cleanliness of the engine and propeller rooms and the simplicity of the direct acting bridge controls, all of which combined to create a very favourable initial impression. This was reinforced by the easy manner in which Augsburg extricated herself from a congested berth and quickly cleared the harbour entrance. Once well out into the lake, Captain Goldsworthy was invited to take over and carry out whatever manoeuvres he wished. Ten minutes at the controls convinced him that here was a system of ship propulsion and control quite beyond compare for vessels engaged in this type of work and for those duties where precision handling and a high degree of manoeuvrability were paramount. Finally, the ease with which the Augsburg could be brought alongside piers and taken off again in a Force 5 wind dispelled any lingering doubts which may have remained and heightened his anxiety to "get in on the act". Following his return to London arrangements were speedily concluded whereby Hardy Tobin & Co., would act as consultants and advisers to Voith in Great Britain. Since they were of the opinion that Voith Schneider propulsion was fundamentally a new method of ship control they considered it would be best handled by a master mariner rather than by a naval architect or marine engineer, and Captain Goldsworthy therefore personally took over responsibility for this new branch of the firms activities. One of the most surprising aspects of the Voith Schneider concept was that, right from the start, it aroused in all those who became intimately involved with this strange device a faith almost amounting to religious fanaticism. Captain Goldsworthy proved to be no exception and returned home wholly converted and eager to preach the VSP gospel to a heathen Britain. From that moment onwards the Voith Schneider propeller was to dominate his whole life!

Theory and Construction

The Voith Schneider propeller consists of a number of vertical blades of aerofoil section symmetrically spaced about a horizontal circular plate (the runner plate) rotating in the base of the metal case housing the drive and control mechanism. When the runner wheel is driven, via shafts and gearing from the main engine, each blade is given a compound motion comprising:

    1) A rotating movement about the axis of the runner wheel.
    2) An oscillating movement about its own trunnion bearings.

The basic law governing the motion of the blades is that the normals to the blade profiles must meet, for all blade positions during each revolution, at one point, the so-called steering centre of the propeller. It is important to appreciate that the 'power' strokes of the blades are made while moving transversely to the direction of motion of the ship, and that they 'feather' when moving parallel to that direction. Fig 3 shows the progressive movement of the path of any one of the blades through the 'power' and 'feathering' positions, but the feather is only of significance when the blade is moving against the direction of water flow. However, as the blade angle on this sweep remains small and only changes very slowly, the resulting drag is relatively slight. On the other side of the sweep the feather position is almost instantaneous as the moving blade 'flips' from a head-out to head-in position very quickly, with thrust coming from both sides of the blade in this movement.

The magnitude of the blade oscillation and its angular direction can be varied by the horizontal displacement of a disc to which the individual blades are connected by a system of levers (fig 4). This linkage has been so designed that a relatively small displacement of the control disc effects a large eccentricity of the steering centre, which is a theoretical, and not a material point in the propeller. When the axis of the disc and runner wheel are coincident the blades merely feather and produce no thrust (fig 5a), but if the disc is displaced transversely either to port or starboard, a thrust is developed and the ship moves ahead or astern (figs 5b and 5c). Similarly, if the disc is displaced longtitudinally a thrust to either port or starboard is produced (fig 5d and 5e). The magnitude of this thrust, which is infinity variable between zero and full power, is proportional to the relative displacement of the disc, thus making the Voith Schneider a variable pitch propeller. Fig 6 shows a cut-away view of the propeller, illustrating the blade link motion, the control disc and the 'joy-stick' by which the displacement of the disc is varied. Two pressure oil servomotors act on the upper end of this centrally pivoted joy-stick, (fig 7) thereby enabling the control disc to be simply moved not only longtitudinally and transversely but in effect also universally swung round the runner wheel axis. The thrust can thus be varied in magnitude and direction horizontally through 360°, thereby enabling the ship to be both propelled and steered by the propeller alone. (fig 5f). The forward/reverse/speed and steering servomotors are operated from a control pedestal in the wheelhouse, the former by means of a lever situated at the side of the pedestal and the latter by a small steering wheel on top. Since the main engines and propellers run at constant speed in a fixed direction of rotation there are no large masses to stop, re-start or reverse and any alteration in the magnitude or direction of the thrust is virtually instantaneous — indeed it is quite possible for a person to be thrown off their feet by the rapidity with which a reversal can be made!

The tremendous advantage of the Voith Schneider over previous vertical bladed propellers is that the thrust can be reversed through the neutral zone, whereas all earlier types had suffered from an unacceptable handicap in that the thrust followed the periphery of the propeller when being reversed from ahead to astern or vice-versa, which gave the vessel a kick to port or starboard during the transition unless the propeller was stopped.

A sectional view of the type of propeller originally fitted to Lymington is shown in fig 8, and a plan of the linkages in fig. 9.

In the case of double ended vessels the superiority of the Voith Schneider system over other methods of propulsion was even more marked, since by positioning a Voith Schneider unit at each end of the vessel it could be made to pivot on its own axis, move sideways under full power, and hold itself up to, or alongside a berth. In addition, since the water inflow speed at the stern is much slower than that at the bow, due to hull friction, the optimum propeller pitch for the stern unit is markedly different to that for the bow. Being variable pitch, both Voith Schneider propellers can be adjusted to absorb their full engine power. Thus, if the total power required to drive a ship at 12 knots is 1000hp, with two Voith Schneider propellers two 500hp engines are required, whereas with fixed pitch propellers these would need to be of 800hp each. Fig 10 shows the operation of a double ended vessel with Voith Schneider units at each end, steering being effected by the stern propeller only when under way. Where slipways are used at terminals the propellers are usually staggered and set back in order to obviate risk of damage, but with correct hull design this has only a minor effect on the overall efficiency.

From the foregoing it can be seen that Voith Schneider propulsion has many advantages, and these can be summarised as follows:

1) The thrust is infinitely variable in magnitude and direction.
2) Thrust and effiency are identical for all thrust directions: the thrust diagram is a circle.
3) Variation in the magnitude or direction of the thrust is instantaneous.
4) The total input power is available for transverse thrusts.
5) Thrust, and hence the ship's speed, is controlled solely by the variable pitch of the propeller.
6) Rudders are eliminated.
7) Steering is completely independent of the ship's speed.
8) The prime mover runs uni-directionaly at constant speed.
9) Choice of engine speed is independent of propeller speed.
10) Control of the ship is direct from bridge to propeller.

Small wonder it has proved to be so popular for vessels required to perform precision manoeuvres in congested or restricted waters. Although Voith Schneider propulsion is best suited to smaller ships of up to about 2000 tons gross and with outputs up to a maximum of 2500hp per propeller, the vessels most suited to benefit are mainly grouped within this range. Open water tests have shown that a Voith Schneider propeller in a correctly designed hull is as efficient as the best open water propeller. Double ended ferries, however, are always less efficient than single ended, but as explained previously this loss is minimised by the use of Voith Schneider propellers. The Voith Schneider propeller is a piece of precision machinery and is therefore higher in first cost than other types, but this is offset by cheaper and less complicated main machinery since any refinements to a normal direct drive, variable engine speed layout, eg. gearboxes and clutches, electric transmission or variable pitch propellers all add considerably to the cost without equalling the versatility of the Voith Schneider installation. Insofar as maintenance is concerned it must be accepted that this will obviously be greater than that required for a fixed pitch screw propeller, but once again this is normally outweighed by the advantages gained, and modern Voith Schneider propellers are much stronger and require considerably less maintenance than the early pattern illustrated in this chapter.

Spreading the Gospel

Captain Goldsworthy tackled his new duties with zeal and energy. His first task was to produce the necessary literature and send it out to all those who would — or should — be interested, and then to follow this up by presenting a paper before one of the learned marine institutions. Glasgow was chosen as the most suitable venue for the latter, not only on account of the large concentration of shipbuilders lining the banks of the River Clyde, but also because the firth, with its large fleets of passenger steamers, appeared to be an ideal area to exploit the advantages of Voith Schneider propulsion. Accordingly, on 19 November 1935 a paper entitled "The Voith Schneider Drive" was given jointly by Captain Goldsworthy and Herr Clerc to the Institution of Engineers and Shipbuilders in Scotland, which aroused considerable interest but no immediate orders. Indeed, it has taken some fifty years for the seed planted at Glasgow by Captain Goldsworthy to bear full fruit. The Voith Schneider propeller did not appear on the Clyde until 1967, and then only as second-hand tonnage, when the former Tilbury-Gravesend passenger ferry *Rose* was transferred north to replace the unique direct-drive diesel-electric paddler *Talisman*. Renamed *Keppel* she still operates a varied programme of Clyde cruises during the summer season. Today, however, of the fourteen passenger ships regularly employed on the Firth, ten are *VSP*, two are double single screw, one is twin screw, and one paddler (summer season only).

Initially, Captain Goldsworthy concentrated his efforts on the shipbuilders themselves, but found they were just not interested. Their attitude was that if the owners expressed an interest in a piece of machinery or equipment they would look into it, but to stick out their necks and actually *advocate* something new — not they! In addition, some of them actually saw the Voith Schneider propeller as a threat, since this would deprive them of work in their own engine shops. Previous short distance passenger vessels and ferries had, in the main, been paddle reciprocating or screw turbine steamers, and the builders thus had a vested interest in maintaining the status quo, since the paddle wheels and steam engines were manufactured in their own yards. A notable exception to this attitude was William Denny & Bros, who were already convinced that the

future lay with the oil engine, and had formed a close association with Sulzer Bros., the diesel engine manufacturers of Winterthur, Switzerland. This experience dictated a change of tactics, and although still maintaining contact with the builders Captain Goldsworthy gradually built up contacts with those owners most likely to be won over by the advantages of Voith Schneider propulsion. His first success came from an unexpected quarter. The United Africa Company had under consideration the construction of a small tug/passenger vessel for service on the River Niger and in April 1936 their representative, Colonel Ratsey, accompanied by Captain Goldsworthy, visited Germany to inspect the Voith Schneider ships on Lake Constance and look over the Voith works. The outcome was that William Denny & Bros., Dumbarton, received an order for the first British built and owned Voith Schneider propelled vessel, and *Katsena,* as the vessel was christened, successfully spent some twenty-seven years towing barges and transporting passengers on the River Niger and its tributary, the Benue. Owing to the Depression, which affected Germany quite as much, if not more so, than Britain, only four propellers were ordered during the whole of 1933 and 1934, but in 1935 a surge of orders resulted in the Voith propeller division being strained to the limit. Senior staff could no longer be spared for field work, but to keep up the UK sales programme Hardy Tobin went well beyond the terms of their agreement with Voith, and on 1 January 1937 a new agreement was reached whereby Hardy Tobin became the Voith Schneider sales agent for the United Kingdom and British Commonwealth.

Throughout 1936 Captain Goldsworthy held discussions with two south coast owners, Red Funnel Steamers of Southampton and the Southern Railway, and by autumn the interest of Red Funnel had been sufficiently aroused to warrant a visit to Germany. This was duly arranged, and in November a party of Red Funnel officials, accompanied by Captain Goldsworthy, visited the Voith works on the 21st. On the following day they joined the *Deutschland* for a cruise on Lake Constance, when they were given every opportunity to study the engine and propeller installation and observe the handling of the vessel at open piers and in the harbours. The interest shown by Red Funnel was matched by the Southern Railway, whose marine staff at Southampton had always received Captain Goldsworthy kindly, and in the early part of 1937 he accompanied Commander Graham and Captain Jefferies, the superintendent marine engineer and marine superintendent respectively, on a visit to Germany similar to that undertaken by the Red Funnel officials. They stayed at a hotel in Friedrichshaven, where in the evening the local manager of the German State Railways challenged Captain Jefferies to a game of billiards. On the outcome of this match depended the futures of the German Railways Southern Section and the Southern Railway in England, since the contestants had decided that nothing less would suffice as the stakes. The result was decisive, with the Southern Railway taking over ownership of the German Railways, although for some technical reason the actual transfer was never officially ratified! Once again every facility was afforded the Southern Railway representatives; a proposed double-ended passenger/car ferry for the Lymington-Yarmouth route was also discussed and although the German Railway authorities had no similar ships in operation they could see no reason why a vessel with a Voith Schneider propeller at each end should not be as equally successful as their own vessels with twin Voith Schneider units aft.

Following these tours Captain Goldsworthy frequently visited Southampton to discuss the new vessels which Red Funnel and the Southern Railway were on the point of ordering. Both were anxious to be the first company to order and put into service a Voith Schneider propelled vessel in British waters, and Captain Goldsworthy sensed the spirit of competition which was developing between the two owners. Both, as has been described in Chapter One, operated competitive car and passenger services to the Isle of Wight and both appreciated not only the operational advantages, but also the resulting kudos, to be gained from being first in the field.

The heathens were gradually becoming converted!

The Influence of Lake Constance

The Lake Constance ships played an important role during the nineteen-thirties in demonstrating to British coastal passenger ship owners the advantages of Voith Schneider propulsion, and in influencing their decisions to choose this system for the new tonnage then under consideration. It is perhaps not inappropriate to consider briefly the reasons which led to the enthusiastic adoption of Voith Schneider propulsion for the lake passenger and ferry fleets from its earliest days. Lake Constance, some 40 miles in length and 10 miles wide, is bordered by Switzerland, Germany and Austria, and lies in an approximate WNW-ESE direction. With the prevailing

SW winds sweeping down from the Alps across the lake the harbours on the NE (German) shore are open to heavy seas which build up very quickly, and all are protected by breakwaters having a narrow entrance and affording only limited space within. In pre-World War II days shipping was one of the regular means of communication in the area, transporting not only passengers, goods and foodstuffs throughout the year but, in addition, having to cope with a very heavy holiday and tourist traffic during the summer months. Passenger ships had to be of shallow draft on account of the winter low water periods and yet have a sufficiently large capacity, within limited length, to provide the spacious, comfortable accommodation so necessary during the busy summer season. With large numbers of tourists and holiday makers disembarking and boarding at the numerous piers, the time spent taking and leaving the piers had to be kept to a minimum in order to maintain schedules, and this combination of navigation and operational problems placed the traditional paddle steamer at a disadvantage. In particular, it was ill-suited to cope with the rapid and precise manoeuvring required within the limited confines of the busy harbours, and for these reasons the shipowners first turned to the twin screw motorship as replacement tonnage, and then adopted Voith Schneider propulsion after its unrivalled manoeuvring and handling qualities had been demonstrated by the *Torqueo*. There can be little doubt that the performance of the Lake Constance vessels was a prime factor in persuading the British shipowners concerned to specify Voith Schneider propulsion for their new tonnage.

Plate 34. (Top left). Ernst Schneider.   E.C.Goldsworthy & Co)

Plate 35. (Top right). *Torqueo* the pioneer motor launch fitted with Voith Schneider propeller.   (E.C.Goldsworthy & Co.)

Plate 36. (Left), Schneider's original model of the propeller.   (E.C.Goldsworthy & Co.)

Plate 37. (Bottom left), *Kempston* on Lake Constance demonstrating her manoeurability.   (E.C.Goldsworthy & Co.)

Plate 38. (Below). The original Voith Schneider Propeller unit as fitted to *Torqueo*.   (E.C.Goldsworthy & Co.)

CHAPTER 3

LYMINGTON

An Unhappy Compromise

At the Southern Railway Board meeting held on 17 February 1937 Sir Herbert Walker reported that Mr Aman's company (The Isle of Wight Ferry Company Ltd.) had been unable to comply with the conditions laid down and had failed to raise the necessary capital within the period stipulated under their agreement with the Southern Railway Company. They had applied for an extension of time but he recommended that this be refused and that the Railway Company now undertake the improvement of their existing service between Lymington and Yarmouth. The General Manager then submitted a scheme which included the abandonment of the present slipway at Lymington, the construction of a slip road and level crossing leading to a new concrete slipway situated at the north western end of Lymington Pier, and the building of a new diesel engined double ended ferry. The new ferry was intended to be capable of dealing with the motor car traffic at present travelling between the mainland and the western end of the Island and also of accommodating the whole of the passenger traffic during the winter months, thus enabling the paddle steamer *Freshwater* to be laid up during that period. The scheme also embodied certain work to be done at Yarmouth by the Yarmouth Town Trust, with the railway company contributing £1000 towards the cost of a new slipway to be constructed there, the total cost of the scheme being:

Work at Lymington	£12,000
Work at Yarmouth	£1,000
New ferry vessel	£27,000
Total	£40,000

Sir Herbert went on to remind the Board that the existing service ran at a loss of about £1500 per year, but that with the probable increase in motor car traffic consequent upon the improved service and the economies effected by laying up the *Freshwater* in the winter a profit of some £3000 was anticipated in the first full year. The motor car traffic between Lymington and Yarmouth had shown only a small annual increase in the last few years owing to the unsuitability of the present method of transit, whereas in the first ten years of operation of the motor car ferries between Portsmouth and Fishbourne the number of cars carried by that route had increased by nearly five-fold. If a proportionate increase between Lymington and Yarmouth took place it would soon necessitate the construction of a second ferry and enable the *P.S. Solent* to be dispensed with. The General Manager concluded by saying that it would also be necessary to provide at Lymington a tractor and trailer costing £750 for the transfer of containers and cargo between ship and trains.

The Board approved the proposals and on the 19th a letter, signed by Sir Herbert Walker, was sent to William Denny & Bros, informing them of the company's decision to proceed with a new scheme for transporting passengers and cars between Lymington and Yarmouth and arranging for the Docks & Marine Manager to visit Dumbarton during the following week to discuss with them a new ferry boat for the service. No doubt Sir Maurice Denny, a man who maintained a regular personal contact with actual and potential customers, was already very well aware of what was in the wind!

The Docks & Marine Manager had already had plans and a specification for the vessel prepared by the marine technical staff and this general arrangement plan, stamped, "Superintendent Mechanical Engineer, Southampton Docks Southern Railway, 25 Feb, 1937" showed a layout very similar to those operating between Portsmouth and Fishbourne. Indeed, the hull itself was identical to that of the three previous ships, but having additional passenger accommodation provided in two sponson houses with open decks above, since it was proposed to operate the winter service solely with the new ship. Propulsion was by means of double twin screws driven by diesel engines, as in the previous ships, but a revision to double twin rudders was made, each pair having its own separate wheel in the wheelhouse, whilst the provision of twin funnels instead of exhaust pipes gave the vessel a much more pleasing aspect than its predecessors.

The meeting with Denny's took place on, or about, 26 February, and discussion centred not only on the layout and specification of the new ship, but also on the navigational problems of the narrow, tortuous and shallow Lymington river. It was explained that Commander Graham and Captain Jefferies had been most impressed during a recent visit to Germany with the performance of the Voith Schneider ships on Lake Constance and as a consequence

were interested in adopting this method of propulsion for their new ship, since it appeared to offer considerable advantages over the double twin screw layout. However, the application of Voith Schneider propulsion to a ship of this type was entirely novel and they were therefore reluctant to commit themselves to it without further independent investigation. Denny's were therefore requested to look into the matter and after much deliberation both at the time and later, eventually came to the conclusion they could use the *Fishbourne* type hull form to accommodate the Voith Schneider propellers, thus enabling them to be easily replaced by double twin screws if found unsatisfactory. Having established this escape route they now felt confident in going ahead and approving the Voith Schneider installation, which, whilst more expensive, undoubtedly offered a number of major advantages over the twin screw layout. In a letter dated 10 March 1937, Denny's wrote to Sir Herbert Walker recommending that the Voith Schneider system be adopted on account of its advantages in manoeuvring, etc., and quoted as follows:

1) Vessel with Voith Schneider propulsion, £29,800
2) Vessel with double twin screw propulsion £27,100

Delivery was promised in time for the vessel to commence the new service on 1 January 1938, subject to the punctual delivery of the propellers and the availability of structural steel at the required time.

Once again, Denny's had come up trumps, for not only had they approved the favoured Voith Schneider system but had also provided an easy and cheap means of converting to twin screws should the Voith Schneider system fail to live up to expectations. The General Manager, with the approval of the Docks & Marine Manager, therefore recommended to the S.R. Board on 17 March acceptance of the Voith Schneider option, and although this received strong opposition from certain directors (on anti-German — not technical grounds) the majority approved the recommendation. The price of £29,800 was accepted in writing on 23 March 1937, the contract stipulating the vessel to be capable of carrying a 45 ton deadweight on a draught of 5'8" at a speed of 11 knots. The Southern Railway public relations department lost no time in announcing that the company had just placed an order for the first Voith Schneider propelled vessel to operate in Great Britain, and under the heading 'Ship without Rudder' the news was widely reported, not only in the Daily Mail, Daily Herald, News Chronicle, Southampton Echo, Manchester Guardian and The Times, but also, of all places, in the Christian Science Monitor!

Whilst the use of the original hull design appeared to be a prudent, cautious and ingenious approach, like so many such 'solutions' it was, in fact, a fudge. It is particularly important with a Voith Schneider installation for the hull form and propeller to be properly matched, and for shallow draught vessels the most favourable arrangement is for the propeller to be mounted vertically, or almost so, under a flat square base. Since Denny's had the *Katsena* under construction at the time they must have been well aware of this, as her stern was specially shaped to meet this unusual requirement. The propellers on the Southern Railway vessel had, of necessity, to be diagonally offset from the longtitudinal centre line in order to avoid being damaged when the vessel ran onto the slipways, but in the Denny layout this not only meant them having to be set well back from the ends but due to the hull curvature also angled outwards at 22½° from the vertical. In this position the blade tips were almost in line with the run of the hull and thus exposed to mechanical damage, whilst in addition undesirable forces leading to bearing failure would be set up in the blades. Voith strongly objected to this arrangement and wrote, "We agree to the general arrangement of the machines and propellers in the ferry, however, we cannot agree to the form of the stern and inclination of the propeller axes". Denny's uncompromising reply was to the effect that any alteration to the hull would adversely affect the required displacement and that the position of the prow hoisting winches precluded any relocation of the propellers.

Thus, in this apparently ingenious design compromise, from which neither Denny's nor the Southern Railway would budge, were sown the seeds which were to bear such costly fruit.

Ship No. 1322

The propeller layout which Voith had been forced to accept was a cause of considerable concern to them and in August 1937 they sent over one of their senior staff (Herr Franz, assistant to Herr Clerc) to examine the actual conditions under which the ship was to operate. His inspection confirmed Voith's worst fears. At low water the Lymington river was little more than a tortuous ditch, and because of

Plate 39. Scale model of *Lymington* and slipway.
(R. Butcher collection)

the position and angle of the propeller blades their tip could well be churning through mud and gravel, causing pitting of the blades, bearing stresses and drawing up sand and silt into the blade seals. Even worse, the shores were full of iron hard baulks of timber embedded in the mud, which dated back to the days when Lymington was an important centre for wooden ship building, and these presented a formidable hazard at very low water when the ship would have to scrape alongside the river banks. It may well be asked why Voith Schneider propellers were recommended, and chosen, in the first place, when the conditions in the Lymington river must have been well known. In fairness to Captain Goldworthy, he never visualised for one moment that the propellers would not be installed in accordance with Voith's recommendations — vertical and inboard from the run of the hull. The Southern Railway men blindly put their faith in Denny's expertise, plus of course their obsession with retaining the twin screw option and their confidence that additional dredging would ensure a safe channel at all states of the tide.

Shortly after Herr Franz's visit and expressed unease, Commander Graham visited Dumbarton to discuss the question of propeller protection, where models of the vessel and the Lymington and Yarmouth slipways were studied to ensure that there would be no danger to the propellers when the vessel berthed. Denny's had allowed for skegs to be fitted in line with the propellers — forward of the fore propeller and behind the aft one — and as a result of the meeting these were now to be located further ahead and astern of the propellers. These skegs served a double purpose; firstly to afford protection when the vessel ran up onto the terminal slipways and, hopefully, to divert any floating logs or baulks of timber away from the propellers, and secondly, to give some measure of course stabilisation. However, in spite of Franz's comments no side protection was added, the only concession in this respect being to increase the width of belting.

Meanwhile, although satisfactory progress was being made on the ship itself all was not well at Voith's. Denny's had ordered the propellers promptly on 27 March and in order to ensure a punctual delivery (7 months) Voith had subcontracted the manufacture of the bevel gears to David Brown, Huddersfield, since the gear cutting machinery at the Krupp works in Germany was already working to full capacity. Unfortunately, David Brown fell badly behind schedule and the gears were not shipped from Goole until 6 November, at lease two months behind schedule, and this delay upset Voith's production schedules, resulting in still further delays. In September, Mr Biddle (the S.R. Docks and Marine Manager) wrote to Captain Goldworthy expressing his disappointment at the inability of Voith to maintain their delivery date and in a further letter dated 4 November pointed out that had the double twin propulsion been chosen then the ship would have been able to enter service as scheduled. As time passed, Biddle became increasingly annoyed, and when in February 1938 news of the latest delay reached him he remarked, not surprisingly, that he was very sorry he had been persuaded to fit Voith Schneider propellers to the new ship as he was having to bear the grave displeasure of his directors over the delays! However, the propellers were finally shipped from Heidenheim, via Zeebrugge-Harwich, on 4 March, and the launch fixed for 1 April — a date considered to be most appropriate by those who had opposed the choice of Voith Schneider propulsion in the first place. Voith suggested that the ship be launched without the propellers in situ, but once again they were over-ruled, this time since no-one was prepared to countenance any further delays in getting the ship into service.

Launch

The policy of the Southern Railway was to use local place names for their Isle of Wight vessels and Ship 1322 proved to be no exception. In spite of the date there were no untoward incidents and at 12.30pm the vessel, christened *Lymington* by Mrs Biddle, at long last slid down the ways into the waters of the Leven. Immediately after the launch, Captain Goldsworthy made a speech from the launching platform and presented to Mrs Biddle a silver salver on behalf of J.M. Voith, whilst as a memento of the occasion Mrs Biddle also received a wristlet watch from the builders. At the lunch following the successful launching Sir Maurice Denny commented that as the vessel would require to navigate the Lymington, a narrow and tortuous river, the Southern Railway Company considered that Voith-Schneider propulsion would provide the best solution to the problem. Such a departure from well established practice was not to be lightly undertaken and he congratulated the Southern Railway on their courage and technical vision. He also remarked that if Voith wished to obtain further orders in this country and to make good progress with the Voith Schneider propeller it was vital that they kept to their delivery dates.

In his reply Mr Biddle said his company had every confidence in the new method of propulsion and they believed it would meet many of the difficulties encountered in navigating the Lymington river. The new ship would revolutionise their transport system between Lymington and Yarmouth and he believed the resulting influx of traffic would soon necessitate them having to worry Sir Maurice Denny and his colleagues with the building of another similar vessel. As an example of how trade followed improved facilities, Mr Biddle referred to the introduction some time ago of an improved service between Portsmouth and the Isle of Wight explaining that in the last year of the old tow-boat system the number of motor cars carried was 1718, while in 1937 it had risen to 24,000. Mr Biddle also stated that they had hoped to have put this vessel into service on 1 January 1938, but owing to the late delivery of the propellers this would now be 1 May.

Plate 40. The Launch.   (Alan Brown collection)

Trials

Lymington had been launched in a virtually complete condition and following a few days final fitting out was ready for sea trials by the middle of the following week. These were scheduled to take place on Thursday 7 April, leaving Dumbarton at 7.00am, and in view of *Lymington's* importance as the pioneer double ended ferry with Voith Schneider propellers, Voith had sent over their chief erector, Herr Schubert, to ensure all was correctly installed and to stand-by during the trials. Naturally, the performance of a vessel with offset propellers was also of great interest to their technical staff, so much so that both Clerc and Franz had come across to assist and observe. Schubert had been supervising the dock trials earlier in the week and was on board *Lymington* at 6.30am on the 7th, waiting to welcome Captain Goldsworthy, Clerc and Franz, who were travelling down from Glasgow by car. Shortly after 6.30am, Mr Russell, the Denny director in charge of the trials boarded the vessel and although aware that the Voith party was due promptly gave orders to cast off.

Arriving on the quayside at 6.45am the three men were astounded to see *Lymington* a couple of hundred feet from her berth, heading downstream towards the River Clyde and obviously on her way to the Gareloch, where the trials were to be run. Their shouted requests for her to heave-to while a launch took them out were ignored, and over a loud-hailer they were told to go down river to Craigendoran pier, headquarters of the LNER Clyde fleet, where she would anchor and pick them up. This cavalier treatment of two top Voith executives infuriated Captain Goldsworthy, and a Denny director who had joined them was informed, in no uncertain manner, of his opinion at such treatment. However, there was nothing else for it but to drive down to Craigendoran where they watched *Lymington* come limping round Ardmore point and slowly steam up towards the pier — something was obviously wrong, but what? Having been picked up

from the pier by the attendant tug, they were welcomed on board *Lymington* with the news that the top labyrinth seal on propeller 115 (which separated and sealed the running and stationary parts), had seized up a couple of miles upstream. Mr Russell had also had time to ruefully reflect on his arbitrary and autocratic action but escaped censure since Captain Goldsworthy and his companions were far too concerned about the propeller breakdown to bother with him—it's an ill-wind . . . . ! Clerc, Franz and Schubert carried out an immediate inspection while the vessel lay at anchor off Craigendoran pier and on emerging from the propeller room, Clerc advised the anxiously waiting knot of people — both Denny and Southern Railway officials were on board — that a repair could be effected within 24 hours of getting back to the yard. The trials were abandoned and *Lymington* headed slowly upstream back to Denny's. This propeller failure greatly worried the builders and owners' non-technical staff, although the engineers were not particularly perturbed, realising the trouble was probably due to insuffient clearance, which in fact was the case. With the assistance of two Denny fitters the three Germans worked throughout the night and following day and by 7.00pm on the Friday evening the propeller had been reassembled and was running under test. All was well, and arrangements were put in hand for the trials to be run on the following day. The magnificent work performed by Clerc, Franz and Schubert greatly impressed Sir Maurice Denny and his co-directors, and also the Southern Railway technical staff, all of whom personally expressed their appreciation and thanked each of the three men for their efforts in effecting a successful repair.

Promptly at 7.00am on Saturday 9 April — this time with *everyone* on board — *Lymington* again headed for the Gareloch, boarded up in readiness for the voyage to Southampton immediately after the trials. This time there were no hiccups, and details are given below:

Plate 41. (Left). The original propeller and stabilising skeg. (E.C.Goldsworthy & Co.)
Plate 42. (Above). *Lymington* on trials in the Gareloch. She is already boarded up for the voyage south. (E.C.Goldsworthy & Co.)
Plate 43. (Below). *Lymington* on her demonstration cruise on 29th April 1938. The original Southern Railway crests and 'Lymington Yarmouth Ferry' can be discerned amidships. (Alan Brown collection)

Trials of MV Lymington
Saturday 9 April 1938

Gareloch: Measured Mile (Bottom ½ mile)

Weather: Fine. Wind: ESE 6 knots. Sea: Calm
Tide: Slack. Commencement of flood.

7.00am Left Denny's Yard, Dumbarton. Proceeded at about 400 rpm engine speed down channel. Swung for compass adjustment off Greenock and proceeded to Craigendoran Pier, arrived 9.20am.

9.45am Left Craigendoran Pier. Proceeded up the Gareloch at full power on the engines, ie 530rpm and full thrust, to the Gareloch measured mile. Draft on leaving, 5'4" forward, 6' aft.

First Run — with engines at full output but with speed lever in arbitary half-speed position, average 7.13 knots on mean of up and down runs.

Second Run — with speed lever at ¾ pitch approx., average speed of two runs up and down, 9.45 knots.

Third Run — with full thrust, average speed on two runs up and down, 11.02 knots.

Fourth Run — with full thrust, average speed on two runs up and down, but with vessel going stern first, 11.09 knots.

Fifth Run — with one engine and one propeller stopped using after propeller only, average speed up and down was 7.86 knots.

The following further trials were carried out:
1. From full ahead to dead stop in water, bringing speed lever back slowly, 22 seconds.
2. With speed lever and ship at full ahead, wheel turned hard to starboard, vessel turned 360° in 1 minute 22 seconds, turning circle 150', ie overall length of vessel.
3. As above, but turning to port, 1 minute 35 seconds, same turning circle.
4. After turning 360° and with full speed turning movement on, the wheel was put hard-over in the opposite direction. Ships head came to rest in 6 seconds.
5. With ship stopped in water, wheel put hard-over to starboard, vessel turned at 360°, pivoting about the bridge in 1 minute 24 seconds.
6. As above, but wheel to port, 1 minute 35 seconds. Various movements to port and starboard were done, but no speed of movement through the water taken. After trials, returned to Craigendoran,   arrived 2.15pm.

2.45pm Left Craigendoran for further ¼ hour, adjusting compass and then ran full speed down the Clyde and back, arriving Craigendoran 4.20pm. Take on stores.

6.15pm Left Craigendoran for Southampton.

On the voyage round to Southampton slight head winds were encountered for the whole way, together with a heavy swell for the first 24 hours, during which time speed was eased back to 7 knots. A heavy swell was also encountered when rounding Lands End but thereafter speed was again increased and at 10.10am on Tuesday 12 April Lymington steamed into Southampton Dock. The voyage coincided with the introduction of Summer Time and allowing for the loss of one hour the actual time in transit was 63 hours, giving an average speed of 9 knots. On the same day she was put into dry-dock, where an examination revealed the propellers to be in perfect condition.

After the dry-dock survey Lymington carried out various trials at Southampton and was demonstrated there on Wednesday 20th to the Chairman of the Southern Railway, greatly to his satisfaction. She then sailed for Lymington, dressed overall, where further trials and manoeuvres were carried out during the afternoon. Experimental trips to familiarise the crew with the vessel and give them practice in handling and berthing were run up to and including Thursday 28th and on the following day Lymington was proudly presented to the press, local dignitaries and other interested parties.

Details

Lymington was the 37th vessel built to the order of the Southern Railway since its formation in 1923, and the 12th for the Isle of Wight services — 8 passenger paddle steamers, 3 car ferries and 1 passenger/car ferry. Her principal particulars are given below:

Hull

Length overall	148ft
Length on car deck	133ft
Breadth moulded	26ft
Breadth extreme	36ft 8ins
Depth moulded	9ft
Max. Load draught	5ft 6ins
Service speed (max)	11 knots

Propulsion Machinery
2 W.H. Allen (Bedford) Type 653OB 4 stroke 6 cylinder oil engines.

Output per engine	200hp
Speed	530rpm max
	500rpm service
Bore	230mm
Stroke	300mm

Propellers
2 Voith Schneider size 12M 80

Diameter of blade circle	1200mm
No. of blades	6
Length of blades	80mm
Propeller speed	230rpm max
	200rpm service

Passenger and Car capacity

Passenger Certificate	Steam 4
Motor Vehicles	17

Passenger Accommodation	Summer	Winter
Ladies Lounge	32	32
Main Deck	316	210
1st Class Lounge	30	30
1st Class Refreshment Room	27	27
3rd Class Lounge	27	27
3rd Class Refreshment Room	27	27
Side Deck Starboard	29	19
Side Deck Port	28	18
Total	516	390
Crew	10	10

With a full load of cars on board the passenger capacity was reduced to 200 in summer and 180 in winter.

For a double ended ferry Lymington presented a quite attractive aspect and was much less utilitarian looking than the three Fishbourne ships, the white upperworks and painted funnels contributing not a little to her more pleasing appearance. The colour scheme was standard Southern Railway marine, viz black hull with yellow lining 3 feet below top of bulwarks, white upperworks, yellow funnels with black tops (Lymington was also given a very narrow black band just below the black tops) and crimson cowl ventilator interiors. The legend Lymington-Yarmouth Ferry in 6 inch black letters, adorned port and starboard navigating bridge bulwarks whilst each sponson house was embellished with a centrally mounted Southern Railway coat-of-arms — a pleasing touch reminiscent of the paddle box decorations on the older steamers. The layout of the vessel is shown in figures 18 and 19 and needs little comment. The bow was identified by the position of the anchor, situated forward on the starboard side, and also by the mast, located on the forward end of the navigating bridge. The positions of the propellers were therefore port forward (no. 114) and starboard (no. 115) — sometimes referred to as B and A respectively. The passenger accommodation in the sponson houses consisted of first and second class lounges and refreshment rooms, together with toilets on the starboard (1st Class) side, as indicated on the drawing of the proposed double twin screw vessel. There was still a considerable traffic in livestock, and pens were provided to seal off a portion of the car deck for this purpose.

Unlike subsequent double ended ferries, which were steered by means of the aft propeller only in order to maintain a forward thrust from the forward one, *Lymington* steered by both propellers. The propeller servo-motors were controlled from a centrally mounted stand in the wheelhouse equipped with:

1) A horizontal steering wheel on top of the stand.
2) A longtitudinally operated speed and reversing lever mounted in a quadrant on the port side of the stand.
3) Two sideways operated transverse thrust levers, mounted in quadrants on the fore and aft sides of the stand.

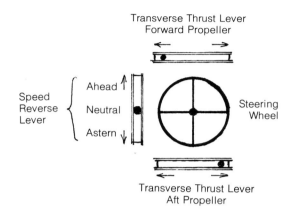

Figure 11. Control Pedestal.

Each transverse thrust lever directed the stream from its respective propeller to either port or starboard, as necessary, when it was required to move the vessel bodily sideways or to spin on her axis without moving ahead or astern. Control of the vessel when under way was via the speed lever and steering wheel only, the transverse thrust levers being used solely for the manoeuvres previously described with the vessel stationary or nearly so, the steering wheel in this case providing the desired degree of thrust. If all this sounds complicated it was in practice quite simple, and although the technique employed by individual skippers varied, all appeared to find the vessel quite easy to control and position exactly as required. Captain Woodgar, her first skipper, remarked "About 15 minutes after I had first taken over control I felt perfectly at home and experienced no difficulty with her". Fifty years later, and with the same controls her two regular Western Ferries' skippers, Captain Ken McArthur and Captain Jim Wilson, effortlessly manoeuvre her onto the link spans at McInroy's Point and Hunters Quay, and have safely taken her across when storms have halted all other passenger traffic on the firth.

Plate 44. The control pedestal. (Alan Brown collection)
Plate 45. (opposite). Captain Goldsworthy and Captain Wilkins (at the wheel) on *Lymington's* Solent trials. (E.C.Goldsworthy & Co.)

Shore Activities

As outlined in Sir Herbert Walker's report to the Board, the modernisation plan for the Lymington-Yarmouth route included not only a new ship, but also for considerable work to be carried out at both terminals, plus the dredging of the Lymington river and approach to Yarmouth Harbour. Following a visit by railway officials to discuss their requirements the Yarmouth Harbour Commissioners wrote to Sir Herbert Walker asking whether in the event of their authorising the necessary works at Yarmouth Quay, at an estimated cost of £6000, they could rely on the company's ferry service from Lymington being maintained for a specific number of years. They also enquired whether the company would be prepared to do this work on their behalf and carry out the necessary dredging at the entrance to the harbour. The Keyhaven episode had obviously left scars, and as Mr Aman was still publicly announcing his intention to proceed with his scheme it is not surprising that the Yarmouth officials were rather cautious. However, on receiving the General Managers assurance that the company had no intention of discontinuing the service, at any rate for a period of at least ten years, and would also be prepared to undertake the reconstruction work at cost price plus 10%, together with the necessary dredging, approval for the work to be carried out was given. This involved the construction of a new concrete slipway, flanked by a timber pier on the eastern side, (foot passengers embarked in the normal manner, and not via the bow ramps) and necessitated cutting off a portion of the old railway Goods Office, a historic building originally associated with Yarmouth Castle. Work commenced in August 1938. At Lymington Pier a certain amount of land reclaimation was necessary for the building of the slipway, connecting road and adjoining car park, whilst for the convenience of rail and foot passengers the pier was widened and the station platform and roof extended, since *Lymington* would berth further upstream than the paddlers. The new pier at Yarmouth was provided with a 7½ ton Cowans-Sheldon swivelling crane for handling the large containers used for the transport of furniture and other through merchandise, whilst at Lymington these were transferred from ship to station on a trailer hauled by an agricultural type tractor. All the required dredging was carried out by the James Dredging Company of Southampton, this work commencing on 7 December 1937.

Demonstration Cruise

Lymington made her special Demonstration Cruise on Friday 29 April, to which members of the press and representatives of local authorities were invited. Among the Southern Railway officers present were J.B. Elliott (Asst. General Manager), R.P. Biddle, S.R. Newcombe (Divisional Marine Manager), Commander W.A. Graham, Captain Jefferies and J.E. Bell (Assistant for the Island), whilst Lymington was represented by Alderman Dawson, (Deputy Mayor), Captain H.H.Lee (Chairman), and others, were present on behalf of the Isle of Wight County Council, together with C. White (Clerk of the Yarmouth Parish Council), H.C. Winsor (Clerk of the Yarmouth Pier and Harbour Commissioners), and other Island interests. Under the command of Captain Wilkins, *Lymington* demonstrated all her party tricks on the crossing from Lymington to Yarmouth, suitably impressing the distinguished audience, and was greeted at the gaily beflagged new jetty at Yarmouth by a large gathering of residents. After disembarking and inspecting the new terminal, guests were then entertained to luncheon at the Royal Pier Hotel. Proposing the toast of "Our Guests", John Elliott, who presided, paid tribute to the splendid co-operation which the Southern Railway had received from the Yarmouth Harbour Commissioners in providing such admirable facilities at Yarmouth Quay. In recent years it had become obvious that the service would have to be improved, especially in the matter of the transport of cars, as the antiquated method of conveying them across in barges towed by a tug was unsatisfactory. On the new service Island residents would be able to purchase a book of six car tickets at the price of four; a concession which he hoped would be appreciated. The new vessel represented a remarkable achievement for which credit was due to the Company's Marine Department as well as to the builders, William Denny & Bros., and he was positive the improved service afforded by *Lymington* would be quite as successful as that between Portsmouth and Fishbourne, which last year carried 24,000 motor cars. As soon as people became fully aware of the improved facilities on the western route to the Island he was confident that the latter would greatly increase in popularity and justify the company's enterprise and foresight.

Alderman Dawson, in his response spoke of the value of the Southern Railway to the ancient ports of both Lymington and Yarmouth and concluded by thanking the company for honouring the town by naming their excellent new vessel after it.

Captain Lee then proposed the toast of the "Southern Railway" and said that the provision of the new slipway and pier had been a big venture for a town of only 800 inhabitants, but they realised that the steamer service was their life blood and that they must do

everything possible to maintain and improve it. A little while ago Yarmouth had been very perturbed to hear that the Railway Company was coquetting with another suitor but they were now delighted that the company had definitely decided to remain true to its old love (hear, hear, and applause). Their only complaint was that the company had not renamed the new vessel "Yarmouth", seeing that it was the second vessel to be given the name "Lymington". However, he believed that the company was so confident of the success of the new service that a sister ship would soon be necessary, which he hoped would be named "Yarmouth".

In his reply Mr Biddle also congratulated the Harbour Commissioners on their enterprise and thanked them for their co-operation. The old towing method of car transport, which had been in operation now for about 30 years was very unsatisfactory, and everyone was delighted that at last it had been replaced by a thoroughly up-to-date and convenient method. They had had it in their minds to name the new vessel "Yarmouth" but that name was already in use on another craft and therefore they were prevented from having it. However, when the sister ship was built, which he hoped would be very soon, they would endeavour to surmount the difficulty. Mr Biddle concluded by stating he felt confident that the improved service, together with the movement for more holidays, spread over a longer period, would be of great advantage to the Isle of Wight.

In contrast to the 24,000 vehicles carried on the Portsmouth-Fishbourne service in 1937, the Lymington route could boast a mere 2,447 cars, plus 213 commerical vehicles over the same period. The hazardous nature of the tow-boat service was highlighted on the 16 July 1937 when Barge No. 4, under tow by the paddle steamer *Solent* and loaded with two private cars and five occupants, one empty lorry and driver, and a small quantity of general cargo collided with the anchored collier *Obsidian* about ¼ mile north of Yarmouth and sank. The passengers managed to scramble aboard a motor launch accompanying the tow but the motor vehicles went to the bottom with the barge and were never raised, although a box containing waterproofs and raincoats was recovered some days later on the beach at Eastbourne. The motor boat, incidentally, was used to manoeuvre the barges onto the slipways at Lymington and Yarmouth when the paddle steamer was used for towing.

Apart from the initial problem with propeller 115 when en route to the Gareloch *Lymington* had behaved in an exemplary manner and proved to be a very seaworthy craft. All was now ready for the new service to commence on Sunday 1 May.

Plate 46. (Above). Chief engineer C. Clark in the engine room. (E.C.Goldsworthy & Co.)

Plate 47. (Below). A lorry and container disembark after the demonstration cruise. The container would be brought by rail to Lymington town station, unloaded there, and shipped via the ferry to Yarmouth, where the goods were either delivered by road, or transhipped onto the Island railway system to a final destination. (E.C.Goldsworthy & Co.)

CHAPTER 4

INTO SERVICE

Lymington proved an instant success. She entered service, as planned, on Sunday 1 May 1938 and on the following day the old Town slipway was closed and the tow boats laid up, marking the end of a 100 year era! Both crew and passengers were full of praise for the new ship and she quickly gained the reputation of being a good sea boat, with plenty of power to cope with the most unfavourable conditions. Captain Wilkins and Captain Woolgar considered her much easier to handle than the paddle steamers, and relished the advantage of not having to turn her in the river off Lymington Pier — no easy operation with a paddle steamer at low water or in blustery conditions. Passengers likewise appreciated the comfort of the electrically heated saloons, tastefully decorated with coloured etchings of local beauty spots by Donald Maxwell, and the uncluttered upper decks from which the imposing chalk cliffs of western Wight could be viewed across the sparkling green waters. The unfamiliar noise and vibration was a small price to pay for such comfort and convenience. Alas, the euphoria was soon to be shattered.

Just exactly what happened is not clear, but on 4 May, when entering Yarmouth harbour, *Lymington* ran her port forward propeller onto what was described as the 'breakwater' — presumably the new pier alongside the slipway. This mishap was not reported, but the propeller had in fact suffered considerable damage and on the 10th the inevitable happened. While berthing at Lymington on the last run of the day the port propeller commenced to shudder, the engineer noted a sudden drop in oil pressure and next morning the level of oil in the propeller casing had risen considerably, indicating entry of water. *Lymington* continued in service for the day, running on the aft propeller only, and on completion of her schedules sailed up to Southampton for dry-docking. It is said that misfortunes never come singly, and in *Lymington's* case this indeed proved to be true; she arrived at Southampton safely enough but then promptly ran her one operational propeller over a buoy while manoeuvring in the dock entrance. This was the last straw — she was berthed in the dock and tied up for the night before anything else could go wrong! When drydocked next morning both propellers were found to have a number of badly bent blades and all showed signs of pitting, due to scouring the river banks at low water. Both propellers were lifted out and partially dismantled, but to assess the full extent of the damage examination by an expert was necessary, and Voith were cabled to send over a fitter as quickly as possible. Back came a telegram bearing the legend:

LYMINGTON. OBERMONTEUR SCHUBERT EINTRIFFT
LONDON HEUTE ABEND MIT FLUGZEUG.

The valiant Schubert was on his way!

Meanwhile because of the Lymington Pier 'red herring' a diver was sent down to examine the slipway but could find nothing which would account for the damage sustained by *Lymington,* and it was therefore assumed that a large baulk of timber must have been caught in the propeller. The truth, that the damage in fact occured at Yarmouth a week earlier, did not emerge until later. To cover the service while *Lymington* was hors-de-combat *Hilsea* was transferred from the Fishbourne run, the first time one of these vessels had been to Lymington.

Obermonteur Schubert duly arrived at Southampton and with the assistance of the German vice-consul and a teacher of German language acting as interpreters was given a detailed explanation of how the damage had been caused — or was thought to have been caused. His subsequent examination of the partially stripped propellers revealed that no apparent damage had been sustained and after the bent blades had been straightened and various bearings replaced the propellers were reassembled and remounted. The work was completed on the evening of Saturday 21 May and at 10.00pm *Lymington* returned to her home base, with Schubert on board to keep an eye on things. Next morning she took over the service, with Schubert still maintaining his watching brief, and at the end of the day he reported that all appeared to be working satisfactorily. Biddle had been extremely anxious to get the vessel back onto the run as quickly as possible, and once again Schubert had worked to the limit to achieve this. Prior to returning to Germany on the 23rd he was thanked personally by both Mr Biddle and Commander Graham for his outstanding efforts.

Two days later *Lymington* was again in the news when she collided with the yacht *Fubbs,* moored in the river between Waterford Lake and the Cocked Hat, and a diligent 'Lymington Times' reporter recorded the *Fubbs* skippers' account of the incident:

"I was rowing away from the yacht at about 9.00am and noticed the *Lymington* coming up river in a normal manner. I was only a few yards from the boat and when the ferry came abeam of the *Fubbs* she seemed to stop dead and her stern swung round, striking the yacht amidships on the starboard side. Had she not been on the mud she would have been sunk."

The cause of the mishap was a failure of the aft propeller, which suddenly lost oil pressure when the spring link on the oil pump driving chain broke and resulted in the stern swinging round out of control. This was not the first breakage, a previous one on the same pump having occured on 3 May, but as the latter happened in open water the consequences were less serious. Nothing of this nature had ever happened on any other VSP ship and it was only after a great deal of investigation that the trouble was finally traced to the pump sprocket itself, which was of too small a diameter for the subdivisions of the roller chain. With three 'incidents' in less than a month the Southern Railway people were beginning to think they had a hoodoo ship on their hands, and awaited with some trepidation the next episode. They were not left long in suspense!

More chickens come home!

Lymington managed a few more days without a mishap but on 3 June it was noticed that water was again entering propeller A. At this point it is perhaps pertinent to explain that the propeller mechanism was pressure oil lubricated, this oil also being used to control the 'joystick' servomotors. In the event of a blade seal failure the oil would be pumped out of the propeller when the ship was under way, and conversely, when berthed overnight, the flow was reversed and sea water forced into the propeller casing. The tell-tale signs of blade seal failure was therefore oil in the wake and a drop in oil level at the end of the day, and an increase in the level the following morning due to the ingress of water overnight. *Lymington* continued in service until 8 June, when a dry-dock became available, and headed up to Southampton in the evening, where propeller A was removed and the aperture blanked off. She berthed overnight in the wet dock and on the following morning the engineer could hardly believe his eyes when propeller B casing now registered an increase in level of 4 inches — water was getting onto that propeller also! Voith had previously been requested to send across an engineer when propeller A had been removed, and on the 9th Herr Heyn duly arrived from Heidenheim. An immediate inspection of the propeller revealed badly rusted internals and some worn blade shaft needle bearings, but nothing to indicate how the water was getting in, since all the seals appeared to be in a reasonable condition. Here indeed was a mystery!

Meanwhile, *Lymington* returned to Lymington and took up her service runs but on the following afternoon, the 10th, severe shuddering was experienced at full speed and when making turns. Southampton was immediately notified but instructions were given to keep going until propeller A was repaired, which proved easier said than done. Some of the necessary spares were not to hand, and to try and make one good propeller out of the two *Lymington* came up to Southampton on the night of the 14th June for propeller B to be removed and cannibalised to provide the parts for A, which had already been cleaned up. On the 17th she returned to service and for two days churned up and down the Lymington river with everyone anxiously scanning the wake for oil leaks and scarcely daring to examine oil levels in the mornings. The coup-de-grace was delivered on Sunday 19th, when the propeller dipstick recorded a marked increase in level. She was immediately withdrawn and quietly made her way back to Southampton on the Monday morning.

Return of the Tow Boats

"Circumstances have arisen which have necessitated the Southern Railway Company's new motor car ferry vessel *Lymington* being withdrawn from service for certain improvements and adjustments which will take about three weeks to complete.

During this period the service for motor cars and general cargo will be performed by a tow boat".

Thus ran the Southern Railway's official statement concerning the replacement of the disgraced *Lymington* by tow boats. As the peak summer season was approaching none of the Portsmouth-Fishbourne vessels could be spared, and the company thus had no option but to re-instate the tow boats, now operating from the new Lymington Pier slipway. Naturally, *Lymington's* departure did not go

Plate 48. *Lymington* demonstrates her maneouvrability on the demonstration cruise. (E.C.Goldsworthy & Co.)

Plate 49. (Right). Unloading at Yarmouth at high tide, showing the necessity for the piles being installed as seen in *plate 26*. The crane on the quay was a legacy from towboat days and had been used to unload containers from the towboats. (Alan Brown collection)

unrecorded in the press, and the 'Lymington Times', in their issue of Saturday 9 July commented:

"Many Lymington people will no doubt be wondering what has happened to the *MV Lymington* which the Southern Railway introduced a short while ago for the purpose of a serviceable ferry between Lymington and Yarmouth. The boat, an innovation and perhaps a novelty to a great number of people, created a nation-wide topic of conversation. Some were optimistic about the craft, some were casual and others sceptical, but at any rate *Lymington* was in the news for a spell, even into the movie news-reel.

The skippers were well pleased with her and declared her to be a wonderful ship. They also said she was easy to handle, but why has the craft not responded to the high expectations of those in charge."

A Silent Departure

"A week or two back the *Lymington* silently went away. There were no gaily coloured flags flying, and there was no publicity as on her first arrival. She just ploughed her way back to Southampton, apparently for further treatment to one of her propellers.

It is only natural that people should take an interest in this particular boat because of her unusual performance and because she was something new and had created a widespread interest in the locality. The Lymington river, from the banks to the bed, form a V and when the tide is at its lowest ebb only a very small amount of water is available for a large boat. This fact was substantiated by the steamboats *Solent* and *Freshwater*. It is also thought that the sharp bend in the river might have a lot to do with the situation and that one remedy would be to dredge the river".

Naturally, the Southern Railway Board had to be notified and at their meeting on 28 June the Docks & Marine Manager was given the unenviable task of reporting that *Lymington* had had to be withdrawn from service due to propeller failure but that it was hoped to effect repairs in time to permit the vessel to return to service on Saturday 1 July.

It was a hope which proved to be wildly optimistic.

Inquest

Perhaps the most mystifying and irritating aspect in the whole sad sequence was that no recognisable reason for the ingress of water into the propellers could be seen, for neither propeller had suffered any mechanical damage nor were there any seal failures. However, Commander Graham's assistant, Mr Liston, a most competent and experienced engineer, suggested that the only way to discover the cause would be to subject the propellers to a pressure test. This was accordingly carried out and water immediately commenced to seep out from fractures in the welding at the top of the blade shaft pots on the main runner wheel. Welding fractures were unheard of on previous propellers of the same type, so what had caused them in the case of *Lymington*? There was universal agreement on this — the heavy blows sustained by both propellers at Yarmouth and Southampton — but in addition it was suggested that the blade shafts may not have been trued up sufficiently accurately and this could well have been responsible for the needle bearing fractures. A mood of cheerful optimism returned and it was anticipated, reasonably enough, that after repairs the problems would be eliminated, but to prevent any recurrence some form of propeller protection must be provided.

In order to get *Lymington* back into service as quickly as possible the original intention was for the rewelding, repairs and reassembly to be carried out in the Southern Railway marine workshops at Southampton, and some initial welding was, in fact, carried out there. However, it was proving difficult to obtain the necessary new bearings, etc., and on reflection the company decided it would be best to let Voith themselves undertake the whole of the repairs since they had the facilities and expertise to ensure a guaranteed outcome. In particular, the welding of the runner wheel blade bearing pots was a very tricky operation if stresses and distortion were to be avoided, and the propellers were accordingly shipped to Heidenheim in late June/early July.

Plate 50. (Left). The original propeller layout and stabilising skeg.
(E.C.Goldsworthy & Co.)

Plate 51. *Lymington* in disgrace at the railway dock, Southampton. (B. Moody)

Skeg Protection

Following the withdrawal of *Lymington* one of the first steps taken was to obtain a spare propeller, and at the Board meeting held on 20 July it was recommended that Voith's quotation of £1450 plus £300 carriage, with a twelve month delivery, be accepted. As it was imperative to have the propeller as quickly as possible, the Docks & Marine manager was instructed to see if the delivery time could be reduced to not more than eight months from the placing of the order. At the same time discussions commenced between Captain Goldsworthy, the SR technical staff and Denny's regarding ways and means of protecting the propellers from damage and one proposal was to shorten the blades by about 6 inches, which Voith agreed was feasible although it would adversely affect performance. They wrote:

"Your proposal to take 6 inches off all the blades gives additional protection from shelving river banks. We must, however call your attention to the fact that the stopping as well as the steering capacity will be considerably reduced. In addition there will be a loss of speed of say ½-¾ knot".

In the same letter they reported on the condition of the propellers received from Southampton:

"Examination of the propeller parts has proven meanwhile that these have been exposed to operating conditions for which they were never intended. The condition of the inlet edges of the wings (i.e., blade tips) shows clearly that these have been operated for some time in heavy gravel banks. The shafts and blades are deformed to such an extent that the deformation can be seen with the naked eye. The re-use of a number of blades is impossible; we have therefore cast and completed a total of 6 new blades.

The condition of the runner wheels and particularly the cracks in the welded seams of the blade bearing pots confirm the effects of abnormal wing forces. No other propellers have shown such damage and there has never been any previous damage with pots or weldings. We are convinced that we will not be able to construct blade bearing pots sufficiently stiff to withstand the stresses prevailing hitherto in the case of the *Lymington*.

The propellers are at present being repaired in our workshops and they will be delivered to you in perfect condition. However we are convinced that we will have dealt only with the effects but not the causes and that after a short time the same troubles will arise again if operated under the same conditions. For this reason we deem it absolutely necessary to remount the propellers in a vertical position as indicated in August 1937".

Naturally Biddle was very concerned at the time involved in carrying out the propeller repairs, particularly as he had informed the Board that *Lymington* would be back in service on 1 July, and on 3 August he wrote to Captain Goldsworthy asking him to impress on Voith the necessity of getting the propellers back to Southampton as quickly as possible. His exasperation then got the better of him and he completed his letter:

"I am sure you will appreciate that owing to the unfortunate series of troubles we have had with the *Lymington* we have lost a lot of traffic. We are also in the rather difficult position of having to 'live-down' the inconveniences to which our passengers have been placed. Should our troubles be repeated in any way when the vessel returns to service we shall most certainly have to consider seriously the substitution of other means of propulsion".

It is easy to sympathise with Biddle, but his remarks really amounted to little more than bluff, since none of the parties involved needed to be reminded of the parable of the mote and the beam. Indeed, at that very time Biddle was on the point of ordering the spare propeller and the question of a Voith Schneider propelled sister ship was being actively considered; had *Lymington* performed in a completely satisfactory manner there seems little doubt that a second '*Lymington*' would have been ordered without question.

In the meantime further consideration was being given to the provision of some form of propeller protection and the Southern Railway had asked Denny's to look into the matter. That sacred cow, the twin screw option, was of course inviolate, particularly as *Hilsea* had shown herself perfectly capable of operating the service successfully, and Denny's therefore merely sought some means of side protection for the propellers. At a conference held at Southampton on 9 August, the possible causes of the damage sustained by the propellers was discussed and the unanimous conclusion reached was that this had been the result of the propellers grinding up against a steep shelving bank of gravel or hard stones either in the Lymington river or at Yarmouth. A discreet silence was maintained on the subject of breakwaters and buoys! Having satisfied themselves as to the cause, in spite of Voith's prediction that the troubles would persist unless the propellers were remounted in a horizontal position, the way was now clear for Mr Russell (Denny's) to offer another piece of fudge. The original fore and aft skegs were to be left in position but additional solid skegs were to be fitted outboard of the propellers. Mr Russell had brought along a wooden model of the skeg which was then placed in position on a model of the *Lymington*, and it was agreed that this would adequately protect the propeller

Plate 52. The Denny protective skeg, showing the aperture which had to be cut to provide a freer flow of water when the propeller was throwing sideways. (E.C.Goldsworthy & Co.)

from sloping side banks and yet not materially affect the speed of the ship — it was even thought that the course keeping ability would be improved. Whether the ship would still be able to move sideways was another matter! However, this could probably be overcome, or partially so, by cutting an aperture in the skeg to permit a less restricted flow of water when thrusting athwartships. Captain Goldsworthy, surprisingly, was in favour of the solid skeg, maintaining that the flow of water from the propeller, when thrusting outwards, would sweep round the sides of the skeg, but both Mr Russell and the Southern Railway staff insisted that he obtain Voith's opinion. Their reply was short and to the point:

"We cannot approve of the propeller protection undertaken by Mr Russell".

Their objections to the Denny skeg were based on four grounds:
1) With a skeg alongside the propeller it could get bent into the blades in the event of a severe blow.
2) Any large logs or baulks of timber floating on or just below the surface could get trapped by the skeg and turned into the blades.
3) The skeg might be buried when going hard into sand or shingle and so not giving the necessary protection.
4) The propulsive efficiency and handling would be adversely affected.

Voith had now resigned themselves to the fact that under no circumstances would the Southern Railway or Denny agree to locate the propellers vertically and they therefore proposed a protective skeg of their own design, which in their opinion, would have the least effect on the propulsive efficiency since there was no blocking or restriction of the race in any direction. A strong fore and aft bar protected the propeller from violent side blows and grounding.

Mr Russell's reaction was to condemn the Voith scheme as being unnecessarily elaborate and more expensive than his own proposal, which he insisted would be as equally effective, and it was decided to go ahead and fit the solid Denny skeg.

The inevitable outcome could have been easily predicted!

More Trials   and Tribulations

The reconditioned propellers finally arrived at Southampton in September, and on Monday 26th *Lymington* emerged from dry dock, complete with the new solid side skegs. Preliminary trials were carried out in the dock, and Captain Goldsworthy's report contained no surprises:

"The *Lymington* was alongside a ship in Southampton Docks and we kept one line out forward and one aft, attached to the ship. The engines were started up and we turned the wheel to starboard. It was found there was no starboard steering effect at all with the speed lever in neutral. With the aid of a small tug we pulled her head out until she was clear of the bows, let go and went slowly ahead. We then turned round in circles inside Southampton Dock. We were unable to get any effect from starboard steering, but the steering to port was the same, or very nearly the same, as before.

We then cast off from the quay, working the ships head out to starboard by going alternatively ahead and astern and proceeded out of the dock into the river. As soon as the vessel was making about 5 or 6 knots there was starboard steering as well as port steering. We then proceeded to clear water and carried out the same trials as were done with the vessel when put into service. The results for both trials are given below:

a) Original trial times
b) Trial times with solid skegs

1) Full speed turn to starboard with wheel hard over (360°)
   a) 1 min. 22 secs.
   b) 3 mins. 31 secs.

2) Full speed turn to port (360°)
   a) 1 min. 35 secs.
   b) 2 mins. 01 secs.

3) Turn on spot 360° starboard
   a) 1 min. 24 secs.
   b) cannot be done.

4) Turn on spot 360° port
   a) 1 min. 35 secs.
   b) 1 min. 40 secs.

5) From full speed to stop
   a) 22 secs.

b) 20 secs.

In addition to the above we carried out a turn of 360° to starboard with the speed lever at full speed but with only ⅔ wheel. The time taken for the turn was 1 min. 59 secs. The effect of the skegs can be summarised:

1) The vessel cannot be turned on the spot to starboard.
2) To turn to starboard the best effect obtained with only ⅔ wheel.
3) Skegs increase resistance to turning.
4) Stopping powers are the same.
5) Steering on straight course improved."

Mr Russell was of the opinion that the Captains would be able to operate the ship successfully with more practice (presumably Denny's would supply tugs for use at Lymington and Yarmouth!), but both Captain Goldsworthy and Captain Jefferies considered the ship to be unworkable and agreed it imperative for aperatures to be cut in the skegs. If this didn't work, then they would have to adopt the Voith design.

Back went *Lymington* into dry dock for these modifications, while Mr Biddle continued to fret and fume at the continual delays. She was ready for further trials on 17 October with results as follows:

a) Original trial times
b) Trial times with skegs having apertures.

1) Full speed turn to starboard with wheel hard over (360°)
   a) 1 min. 22 secs.
   b) 1 mins. 48 secs.

2) Full speed turn to port (360°)
   a) 1 min. 35 secs.
   b) 1 mins. 54 secs.

3) Turn on spot 360° starboard
   a) 1 min. 24 secs.
   b) 2 mins. 08 sec.

4) Turn on spot 360° port
   a) 1 min. 35 secs.
   b) 1 min. 27 secs.

5) From full speed to stop
   a) 22 secs.
   b) 27 secs.

This was much better!

Satisfactory berthing trials were then carried out at Yarmouth and Lymington and on the following day similar trials were carried out with Captain Wilkins in command (Captain Woolgar had taken her out the previous day) after which it was agreed that she could return to service on Monday 24 October.

The trials and tribulations were over — or were they?

Lymington II

In spite of *Lymington's* long period out of service traffic on the Lymington-Yarmouth route had shown a marked increase and on the conclusion of her satisfactory trials the Southern Railway again raised the topic of a second double ended ferry for the route. Denny's were asked to submit a complete proposal and price for a vessel similar to *Lymington* and having Voith Schneider propellers fore and aft, but as delivery could not be guaranteed until October 1939, after the end of the peak season, the railway company decided not to proceed for the time being.

More modifications

Lymington duly returned to service as planned on 24 October and initially all went well, but it was not long before all the old troubles again manifested themselves. No breakwaters or buoys were run over, but blade pitting, bearing and seal failures and fractured blade shaft pot weldings continued to plague the vessel, and in January *Lymington* had again to be withdrawn. At this time of the year one of the Fishbourne vessels could be easily spared, and *Fishbourne* was sent down to cover the service. *Lymington's* absences were now no longer newsworthy, and in the absence of the bridge logs for the period it is rather difficult to ascertain just how long she was out of action. However, on 31 January 1939 a meeting was held at Southampton to try and identify the causes of the further propeller failures and decide what action should be taken to overcome these. In addition to Captain Goldsworthy and members of the Southern Railway marine technical staff, representatives from Denny Bros and Voith were also present and in spite of Mr Biddle's previous threats that serious consideration would have to be given to substituting alternative means of propulsion in event of further trouble it is interesting to note that this option was not even mentioned! Three possible causes were put forward by Captain Goldsworthy and Herr Heyn (Voith):

1) Stresses set up in the runner wheel due to the effects of welding carried out at difficult times on the blade shaft pots.
2) Close proximity to the propellers of the existing side skegs which cause reaction forces on the blades and set up blade vibration.
3) Touching of submerged objects, which although not causing excessive blade distortion may have set up blade vibrations.

Herr Heyn then remarked that the best method of overcoming the problem would be to relocate the propellers in a vertical position but if the company were not prepared to do this then the present skegs should be replaced by the Voith design. Once again the proposal to mount the propellers vertically was ignored and the following measures were agreed:

1) To shorten each blade by 6 inches.
2) To replace the existing side protection skegs by those designed by Voith.
3) To secure the services of a Voith welder to carry out the necessary rewelding in this country.

This work was duly carried out, and *Lymington* returned to service in late February/early March 1939. Fortunately the spare propeller was delivered before the outbreak of war, and this proved to be a godsend, since a faulty unit could now be replaced by the spare and then repaired at Southampton in readiness for the next change. Having to go up to Southampton for dry-docking each time a propeller required changing was an inconvenient, time-consuming and expensive business and a technique was developed whereby the spare propeller was taken down to Lymington on a flat bed lorry and run onto the ship. The vessel then proceeded round to the back of the pier, which dried out on the ebb, and the propeller was changed while the vessel sat on the mud. *Lymington* then returned to the slipway on the rising tide, where the lorry disembarked and conveyed the faulty unit back to Southampton for repair. The operation was normally carried out overnight after the vessel had come off service and usually took about 6 hours once the vessel was on the mud, although unfavourable tides meant the vessel could be out of service for 24 hours or even longer.

E.C. Goldsworthy & Co.

Captain Goldsworthy's concentration on the Voith-Schneider propeller had made it difficult for him to devote much time to other business in the partnership and it was understandable that his two associates were becoming rather restless, particularly as this side of the business was running at a financial loss. The agency territory was rather unique in that the shipowners and shipyards were scattered all round the coast, necessitating heavy expenditure in maintaining contacts, seeking orders and following these up during the construction and commissioning periods and after entering service. Under the circumstances it was essential for a new contract be drawn up with Voith if Hardy Tobin & Co., were to continue to act as their agents, and revised terms were agreed which came into force on 1 January 1939. However, with five British owned Voith Schneider vessels now building or in operation and thereby attracting more and more interest in this method of propulsion it is not surprising that Captain Goldsworthy was finding it almost impossible to deal with anything other than Voith Schneider matters. His partners contended that he was devoting virtually all his time to something, which, in the event of war and the current anti-German attitudes, was not likely to result in much hard business and thus add to the gross income of the partnership. As for Captain Goldsworthy, let him continue the story in his own words:

"For my part, I was immersed and caught up in the affairs of the Voith Schneider propeller, in looking after the vessels we had in service, in keeping up the sales pressure, in discussions and appointments and in writing papers to learned societies, including one for the British Association to be delivered at Dundee in September 1939. I could not, therefore, draw back even if I had wished to do so and in consequence it was mutually agreed to dissolve the partnership and for me to commence business on my own with the Voith Schneider propeller, provided Voith were agreeable. We submitted the proposal to Voith, who gave their consent and arrangements were made to start my own business on 1 September 1939. I found myself two delightful rooms in Norfolk Street, just off the Strand, and my secretary, Betty Kennett, was more than willing to come with me since she, too, had got bitten with the Voith Schneider bug."

During August, while the new premises were being redecorated, Captain Goldsworthy was at Dundee attending the commissioning of the *Abercraig* and when war was declared on 3 September he immediately returned to London on the overnight train. Arriving at Euston he first took a taxi to Norfolk Street, went up to his new offices, put his brand new key in the door and said to himself: "Well, this is the way to open a business . . . .", and, turning on his heel, shut the door, and said " . . . .and this is how to close it!

Would he, he wondered, ever open that door again?

Plate 53. Back in service. Coming up the Lymington river in 1939
(late F.A.Plant)

Plate 54. (Below). The Voith designed protective skeg.
(E.C.Goldsworthy & Co.)

Plate 55. Lymington pier with *Lymington* at the slipway and *Freshwater* in the background. (Alan Brown collection)

Plate 56. (Right). The Voith Schneider propelled *Abercraig* on trials on the Clyde. The general layout of her paddle predecessors was followed, but with over double the space for cars. Passenger accommodation was very limited on the Tay vessels, much of that traffic went by rail over the famous Tay bridge.
(Allan T. Condie collection)

Plate 57. One of *Abercraig's* unique eight cylinder Blackstone-Brush 450hp horizontally opposed diesel engines. These enabled an engine room height of 6'6'' which greatly aided the attainment of a loaded draught of only 5'1'', essential to get over the 'Middle Bank' at low water. All three pre-war British Voith Schneider passenger/vehicle ferries were remarkable for their quite different design concepts. (Allan T. Condie collection)

CHAPTER 5

WAR-TIME – AND AFTER

Apart from the blackout the outbreak of war initially marked little change in routine on the Lymington-Yarmouth run and *Lymington* continued to maintain the service as usual over the winter months. However, in the Spring of 1940 the 'phoney war' suddenly became a real one as Hitler's Panzers swept across France and the British Expeditionary Forces had to be hastily rescued from the Dunkirk beaches. Of the Lymington fleet *Freshwater* alone was commandeered to assist in the evacuation and afterwards continued in naval service as an examination vessel, based at Weymouth, until April 1944. *Solent* remained at Lymington on relief duties, although one of the Portsmouth - Fishbourne ferries usually took over in the event of any lengthy absence on the part of *Lymington*, such as annual overhaul.

Following the loss of the PS. *Portsdown*, mined off Southsea in September 1941, *Solent* transferred to the Portsmouth-Ryde route and remained there until the end of the war.

With France now in German hands enemy air activity in the Solent area, which included minelaying, became an ever present hazard and the Isle of Wight was made a restricted area, out of bounds to all except residents and military personnel. *Lymington* received an overall coat of naval grey, plus degaussing cables for protection against magnetic mines, and with a machine gun mounted on the bridge to afford some measure of defence against air attack continued to carry the scanty civilian traffic, including a daily goods delivery service by railway lorry to west Wight, together with an increasing amount of military traffic. Normally, no sailings were made during the hours of darkness, and after overnight Luftwaffe operations in the area *Lymington* was not permitted to sail until minesweepers had been through the Solent. In addition, some crew members were detailed for nightly fire-watching duties but in spite of the military presence in the area neither ships nor pier suffered any bomb damage. The slipway facilities at Lymington and Yarmouth permitted large numbers of military vehicles to be transported to and from the Island and the importance of the route can be gauged, for example, from the relief of the 12th Infantry Brigade by the 214th in December 1940. The whole operation took nine days, during which *Lymington*, assisted by *Wootton*, conveyed some 5,570 men and 544 vehicles across the Solent, no mean feat when one considers the total capacity of the two ships amounted to no more than 32 small vehicles per trip and much less when lorries were carried. In April 1942 as preparations began for the eventual Allied landings in France the slipway at Lymington pier was widened to accommodate two landing craft, and it became commonplace for *Lymington's* crew to find three or four American landing craft moored off the pier in the mornings.

Luftwaffe Attack

Lymington had the honour of being singled out for attack by the Luftwaffe on 10 August 1942 when a lone German raider machine gunned her in mid-Solent. Chief Engineer Fred Howland recalls the memorable occasion:-

"I was sat down in the engine room, along with the greaser, at the time and suddenly something fell down at the bottom of the engine room ladder. We got up and found it to be the glass cover off an electric light fitting, so we went up top and found a hole where a bullet had gone through the bulkhead and knocked off the light fitting at the engine room entrance. That bullet actually ended up in the engine room but another went through the seat of a bicycle leaning against the ship's side. Of course, we hadn't heard a thing down in the engine room and had no idea of what had been going on."

In fact, quite a lot had been going on, and at the first sign of trouble, when the aircraft swooped down towards *Lymington*, Deck Hand G. Sticklee dashed onto the bridge to man the machine gun and this quick return of fire may well have prevented the attack from being pressed home. Mr Sticklee was subsequently warmly praised for his prompt actions and devotion to duty and received a number of official letters of commendation, including one from the General Manager, Eustace Missenden, which is reproduced here. *Lymington* was obviously not a vessel to be trifled with and no further attempts were made by the Luftwaffe to liquidate her; presumably, Goering must have warned them to keep well clear of this strange vessel!

At the time of the D-Day landings, all civilian traffic ceased without notice and the slipway and pier were used entirely for troop embarkation — in any case there was hardly space in the Solent for a vessel to get across to the Island — and *Lymington* went up river on the top of the tide to tie-up off the old slipway, the only time she ever ventured beyond the Pier. Although Lymington played its part in the invasion preparations it never attained the same importance as Southampton or Portsmouth on account of the restrictions imposed by the river and after the successful Normandy landings and establishment of bridgeheads *Lymington* reverted to her normal daily activities.

Plate 58. Streaked and battered, *Lymington* soldiered on throughout the war. Here a load of fairground equipment is being carried to the island. (Alan Brown collection)

Plate 59. In wartime grey, note the concrete protection atop the wheelhouse which required extra supports to be fitted. (Alan Brown collection)

Plate 60. *Vecta* was on her pre-service demonstration cruise. Her conventional lines belied the fact that she was Voith Schneider equipped. Cars were carried on the enclosed foredeck and loaded in the same way as the paddle steamers through side doors.
(T. Cooper Collection)

Vecta

It will be recalled (Chapter 2) that in addition to the Southern Railway representatives a party from the rival Southampton company had also visited Lake Constance and the Voith works at Heidenheim. Cyril Sharp, the Red Funnel Steamers general manager, served in the Royal Flying Corps during World War 1 and in 1917 had been shot down behind the German lines, was rescued seriously injured from the wreckage, taken to hospital and with infinite care nursed back to good health. During the visit to Heidenheim he learned that his Voith host, Gunter Franz, had been a flyer in the Austrian Air Force at the same time and had also been wounded and brought down. With so much in common it is not surprising that the two men quickly took to each other, and this cameradie engendered a most cordial and relaxed atmosphere between the parties. Such encounters can do much to influence decisions and combined in this case with the very favourable impression created by the Lake Constance ships, it came as no surprise to learn that the new Southampton - Cowes vessel ordered from John I Thorneycroft & Co Ltd., Southampton in April 1937 was to have Voith Schneider propulsion. Although ordered only one month after Lymington, it was not until 14 July 1938 that the new ship, christened *Vecta* by the Hon Mrs Pleydell-Bouverie, entered the water, and as a memento of the occasion she was presented with a handsome drinking mug — one does rather wonder just what the elegant, charming and sophisticated Mrs Pleydell-Bouverie thought of her 'handsome drinking mug'. At the luncheon held afterwards Sir John Thorneycroft remarked that Red Funnel Steamers, unlike many other shipowners, did not place their orders abroad, neither did they have their vessels built in other parts of the country, they preferred to have them constructed locally — the fact that Sir John also happened to be a major shareholder and director of Red Funnel may perhaps have had some influence on where their ships were built! Insofar as the Voith Schneider propellers were concerned, Sir John contented himself with the bland remark that the propulsion system was one of considerable technical interest and *Vecta's* performance would be watched with interest by shipbuilders and shipowners alike. In his response Mr Cyril Sharp hinted that not all the directors and shareholders approved the use of German Voith Schneider units but that officials of the company who had visited Germany took with them the master who would have charge of the new ship and who, as a result, was most enthusiastic about Voith Schneider propulsion.

Trials were run on 14 and 15 February 1939 off Stokes Bay when a speed of 15.41 knots was attained. As in the case of *Lymington*, overheating of the main labyrinth seal on a propellor occurred and this prevented her from being handed over to the company until Tuesday, 7 March. After spending some time on pre-service familiarisation runs between Southampton and Cowes the Press were invited to a demonstration cruise on Thursday, 23 March and *Vecta* entered service a day or two later. It would be fair to say that in those days the Red Funnel vessels were designed primarily as passenger ships with some accommodation for cars, rather than the reverse, and *Vecta* followed this tradition faithfully. Fig. 18 shows the general layout of the ship, and the flat underbody at the stern for the twin Voith Schneider propeller mountings can be clearly seen. She soon proved to be a favourite, not only with the master, officers and engineers because of her manoeuvrability in the sometimes crowded and congested Southampton Water and Cowes Roads, but also by passengers who welcomed the up-to-date comforts and convenience.

After the outbreak of war, Captain Goldsworthy first spent some time with the Fleet Fuelling Service at Devonport and then moved to Slough as Research and Development Officer with the firm of High Duty Alloys Ltd. In this position he was able to maintain contact with Lymington, Vecta and Abercraig (the Tay ferry which entered service in October 1939) although of course, all communications with Heidenheim had now ceased. The Southern Railway engineers, headed by Commander Graham and his assistant, Mr Liston, were able to maintain the *Lymington* propellers in good order and thus enabled her to operate throughout the war in spite of bouts of blade and bearing damage. The excellent facilities and equipment of the Southampton marine workshops, together with Mr Liston's expertise, enabled all parts to be fabricated by the Southern Railway themselves, whilst replacement seals were obtained from specialist seal and packing manufacturers. Mr Player, engineering director of Fleming & Ferguson, Paisley, the builders of *Abercraig*, admirably maintained the Tay ferry and only *Vecta* became a casualty. In view of the many misconceptions and rumours which have circulated concerning the Red Funnel ship, and still do, it is perhaps time to put the record straight, and to consider in detail what actually happened. In January 1942, some three years after *Vecta* had gone into service, Captain Goldsworthy received a telephone call informing him that water was entering both propellers, and subsequent inspection showed the bottom plates of the runner wheel in both propellers to be badly corroded and holed, thus letting in water, a condition which would not have happened had they been carefully examined annually and the anti-corrosion zinc anodes renewed as necessary. Since salt water had been in the propellers for a few days it was considered advisable to strip them for a complete examination, which revealed all internal parts and roller bearings to be in excellent condition and with no more wear on the main seal surfaces than would be normal after three years continuous service. Apart from dressing some of the white metal bearing surfaces of the main thrust plate and renewing some broken carbon segments in the stuffing box, no further work on the internal mechanism was necessary, which makes an interesting comparison with that of Lymington. *Vecta's* two propellers were, of course, correctly mounted, with only a very slight inclination aft, and although she had not to negotiate a shallow winding river there was nevertheless a certain amount of silt and sand churned up during the low water periods.

Thorneycroft's had no experience in the repair of Voith Schneider units and at the time were working to full capacity on naval contracts. In view of this, Captain Goldsworthy strongly recommended the Southern Railway be approached with a view to letting them carry out the necessary repairs, which involved making and welding up new runner wheel plates, a particularly tricky operation since it was vital for the shaft bearing pots and stiffeners to be welded in precisely the correct position and absolutely square to the runner wheel. Any distortion caused by welding stresses would quickly result in a seriously damaged propeller, hence Captain Goldsworthy's earnest pleas to have this work carried out at the Southampton marine workshops, which had already successfully undertaken such repairs. Sir John, however, wouldn't hear of it — "No, no, we can do the work here", and do it they did. No sooner had *Vecta* returned to service than Captain Goldsworth received another telephone call — water again in the propellers — and once more the units were stripped, this time to reveal rusted and chewed up blade shaft needle bearings. Unfortunately all the Voith spares had been destroyed in an air-raid and it was decided to replace the needle rollers with plain bearings, but probably due to distortion of the blade bearing pots and damage to the internal mechanism caused by this the propellers could not be successfully reassembled. *Vecta* was then permanently withdrawn and laid up until the end of the war, when she was converted to normal twin-screw propulsion with diesel-electric drive. Captain Goldsworthy remained adamant that had the propellers been sent to the Southern Railway in the first place they would have been renovated and reassembled correctly and *Vecta* would have retained her Voith Schneider propellers to the end of her days. As it was, due to lack of proper maintenance and a reluctance to have repairs carried out by those with the 'know-how' to do the job properly, the owners not only lost the use of the ship for some three years but were then faced with an expensive conversion when peace returned.

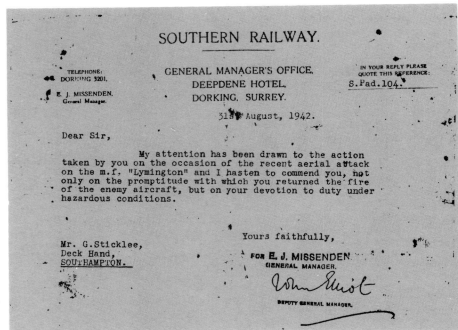

Plate 61. Copy of the letter of commendation.

Picking Up The Threads

As soon as possible after the cessation of hostilities in Europe Captain Goldsworthy made arrangements via the Shipbuilding Conference and good offices of Sir Amos Ayre to visit Heidenheim as an investigator and to report back on the present situation of the Voith Company, including any further developments in the Voith Schneider propeller which may have taken place during the war. In order to visit Germany at that time it was essential to have some form of military standing, and he was given the rank of Colonel (unpaid) — a very rapid promotion from Private in the Home Guard! "Colonel" Goldsworthy was surprised to find Heidenheim and the Voith works standing intact and undamaged, and after making his presence known to the Town Major — an American, since Heidenheim was in the American Zone — hurried to the Voith works, where he was received with much warmth by Gunter Franz and Dr Hans Voith. Eventually the question was raised "How had Heidenheim and the Voith works survived intact amidst such devastation". Dr Voith admitted that he too had been mystified (but eternally grateful) and had assumed that the lack of bombing had been due to their excellent camouflage making it difficult for the planes to pick out the precise targets. However, after the Americans had taken the town he had remarked to the General, "We have been singularly fortunate in that we have not been bombed here". The American agreed, and then spread out a set of photographic maps of Heidenheim and the Voith works for Dr Voith's inspection. There, to his utter astonishment was a detailed layout of each individual workshop and, in addition, precise notes on what each machine was being used for. The General then explained that the Voith works had been spared any bombing because their activities at that time were not making any major contribution to the war effort and, of equal importance, they wished to have the full use of the factory and workforce for the repair of bridges, locomotives, rolling stock and heavy lorries in order to re-establish the general transport facilities in Southern Germany when hostilities ceased. As for the camouflage, the general agreed that it was 'pretty' but nevertheless had been a completely ineffective concealment!

The knowledge that the Voith combine had survived the war virtually unscathed sharpened Captain Goldsworthy's resolve to return to business on his own account and by the end of 1945, all the necessary arrangements had been made. Suitable office accommodation had been secured — no easy matter in those days — and on 1 January 1946, he commenced operations from 7, Victoria Street, London as an independent consultant and prospective agent for Voith when propeller production eventually resumed. A further visit to Heidenheim was made in March 1946, when he was disturbed to find Dr Voith gravely concerned about the future prospects for the Voith Schneider propeller, since it had been a financial loss to the company so far and majority opinion was that it would be better to cut their losses now and not resume production even when given permission to do so. Captain Goldsworthy counter-argued that in the foreseeable future there would be a considerable demand for the specialised type of ship for which the Voith Schneider propeller was ideally suited and cited as examples the enquiries he had already received and the interest again being shown. For Voith to jettison the whole concept now would, in his opinion, be quite wrong and open up the distinct possibility of some other firm marketing the propeller and thus benefitting from the two million marks research and development programme carried out so far by Voith. Whether Captain Goldsworthy's words were based more on emotion than a disinterested appraisal is perhaps a matter for debate, but in the event his predictions proved to be correct, although taking longer to fructify than was thought at the time. Eventually, in no small measure due to Captain Goldsworthy's imperturbable confidence and persuasive argument, Dr Hans Voith took the decision to go ahead and production resumed in 1948. With the post-war development of the propeller now assured, and as agent for Great Britain and the Commonwealth Captain Goldsworthy once again vigorously — 'aggressively' I believe is the modern term — set about the task of publicising the propeller and establishing contacts both old and new in the search for VSP business. One of the first orders received was from a pre-war customer, the Dundee Harbour Trustees, who early in 1949 decided to have a sister to the *Abercraig* built by the local Caledon Shipbuilding & Co Ltd.

Plate 62. *Lymington* back in pre-war livery, but still with the concrete wheelhouse top supports, which would not be removed until her next refit.   (Alan Brown collection)

Paddle Motor Vessel LYMINGTON

To return to *Lymington*. Although the Southern Railway had maintained the propellers in good order throughout the war, the general impression current at the time was that the Voith works had been badly bombed and that spares or replacements were unlikely to be available for some considerable time, if ever. With an anticipated life of around 25-30 years still ahead of her the question of whether or not to retain the Voith Schneider propellers had to be faced and after some discussion on the subject Mr Short, the acting Docks & Marine Manager, wrote to Denny's in May 1945 informing them that as *Lymington* was still suffering frequent propeller damage due to the navigational problems of the Lymington river they proposed to replace the existing Voith Schneider propellers with paddle wheels, and requested them to look into this proposal. The supreme irony of this was that now, after 8 years of endless trouble due to insistence on retaining a hull form suitable for conversion to double-twin screw propulsion, they now proposed to use paddle wheels. Surprisingly, Denny's never batted an eyelid at this bizarre scheme but calmly went ahead with their calculations and on 21 May 1945 wrote to the Ministry of War Transport Marine Surveyors Office in Glasgow intimating that they had been asked to look into the question of converting the *MV Lymington* to paddle propulsion. Approval was therefore sought for an increase in the load draft of 5 inches due to the increased hull and machinery weights. The surveyor agreed to this provided the vessel was not employed outside Steam 4 certificate limits. It was doubly ironic, therefore, that whereas an increase in draft to permit the Voith Schneider propellers to be installed vertically had been quite impossible in 1938, it was now quite feasible to increase the draft by 5 inches to accommodate paddle wheels!

Denny's assumed that with a total engine output of 400 HP and a transmission efficiency of 85% 340 HP would be available at the wheels, giving a speed of 10.5 knots at 45 rpm. Paddle wheels of 12ft 8ins diameter and fitted with 7 flat steel flats 8ft 6ins by 2ft 9ins were to be used, with the curious provison that should wooden floats be fitted the outer edge must not be bevelled but left square or slightly rounded over. The star centre setting gave equal feathering in both directions. It is not clear what type of transmission was visualised, but whether electrical or mechanical an efficiency of 85% sounded decidedly optimistic. Why the simpler and much cheaper double twin screw option had been discarded is again not clear, particularly as *Fishbourne* and her sister, although certainly under powered, had apparently proved quite successful on the run.

The Southern Railway's intention was to withdraw *Lymington* from service on 1 October 1945 for conversion during the forthcoming winter months and to have her back in service by Easter 1946. However, after the initial discussions and investigations everything went quiet, October came and went, and *Lymington* continued to plod between Lymington and Yarmouth as usual. Although all speculation is said to be idle the project was so intriguing that some thought concerning its failure to materialise does seem to be justified. At that time, due to shortage of steel and other materials and the tremendous demands being made on the shipbuilding industry, it is quite possible that permission to virtually rebuild an already operational vessel was refused. On the other hand if the conversion would be too expensive or complicated why did the railway company not opt for the double twin screw option? Perhaps, one day, some intrepid researcher, well equipped with explosives, hydraulic rams and oxy-acetylene cutting gear may eventually penetrate the dark, sealed dungeons of the National Maritime Museum and succeed in liberating the legendary "Denny Collection". All may then be revealed!

Plate 63. *Farringford* was much larger than *Lymington* but could not be complimented for her good looks. She is seen here in original condition with single short mast and short exhausts.
(Alan Brown collection)

A Reversion to Paddles

The first proposals for the re-establishment of the Southern Railway fleet when peace returned were formulated in 1943 when a Joint Committee of the General Council of British Shipping and the shipbuilding industry was set up to explore ways and means of avoiding the boom and slump which had followed the previous war. The four main-line railway companies were invited to estimate their demand on the shipbuilding industry in the immediate post-war period on the basis of the losses suffered up to that time (1943) and the replacement of obsolescent tonnage and vessels not worth reconditioning. The Southern Railway returns for the Isle of Wight services included a single new car/passenger ferry required for the Lymington-Yarmouth route. Strictly speaking, this was not to replace war losses but could be broadly interpreted as a successor to the paddle steamer *Solent*, which after all had been used to tow car-carrying barges in the pre- *MV Lymington* days. The details given were for a vessel 148 ft in length, and of 275 gross tons burthen, diesel engined with Voith Schneider propulsion and were obviously based on *Lymington* although it was stressed that when the time came to place orders for the new tonnage the Southern Railway were in no way committed to the particular type of hull, machinery or propulsion outlined above and that the Board would be free to review the requirements at that time in relation to the most

recent advances in technical design and practice. In their suggested priority for the new vessels the Lymington ferry headed the list in conjunction with two Southampton based cross-channel vessels, with 1945 given as the order date. It was therefore one of the first vessels to be considered, and the manner of its conception is described by Leslie Harrington, the Assistant to the General Manager at that time:

"The decision to revert to paddle propulsion was not prompted by any disenchantment with the Voith Schneider propulsion; during the war, with no German assistance available, the superintendent engineers of the Southern Railway and their staff with typical British pragmatism quickly learned to deal on their own with its occasional teething vagaries. I well recall the occasion when as assistant to the general manager, I was asked to visit Dumbarton with the superintendent engineer and marine assistant to discuss with Denny's their ability to undertake the building of the new vessel. We travelled on the night sleeper from Euston, and after breakfast we boarded a bus for the 15 mile journey to the shipyard.

I said to my colleagues that while we were primarily concerned with yard capacity in the difficult post-war conditions, we should have an idea to put to the shipbuilders.

Plate 64. A two ship service! *Lymington* unloads at Lymington while *Farringford* lies alongside the Railway pier. (Alan Brown collection)

We knew that the Voith-Schneider works were badly damaged by allied air raids, and that form of propulsion was out of the question for the immediate future. So, there and then, we set out to design the ship that became the *D.E.P.V. Farringford,* the only paper available being the back of a large envelope in my briefcase.

When we were received by Sir Maurice Denny in his office, I showed him our sketch. He replied "certainly Denny's can quickly build such a vessel; but first let me arrange for you to go over to Queensferry Passage which we are operating for the London and North Eastern Railway. Your rough drawing is basically an improvement and refinement of our vessels." Capt. Jefferies, the marine assistant, took the wheel of one of the ferries to test her capability, weaving in and out of the piers of the Forth railway bridge, much to the amazement of the passengers, including an air-vice-marshall. This manoeuvre, we were told later, was strictly forbidden by the harbour regulations.

Was there ever another vessel the outline design of which was prepared on the back of an envelope on the top of a bus? Yet a successful one, a far cry from the times, which I can just remember when the older paddlers at low water spring tides sometimes hoisted a foresail to assist them in the Lymington River."

Mr Harrington was, of course, wrong about the Voith works, but the effect was the same — Voith Schneider propellers were unobtainable and the choice therefore lay between paddle or double twin screw, although unfortunately he failed to mention why the double twin screw system had been discarded in favour of paddle. One possible explanation is that the new ship was to be much larger than *Lymington* and paddle propulsion enabled the draft to be minimised.

Although the two Denny ferries operating on the Forth had diesel-electric propulsion, Denny's were by no means enamoured with this form of drive, considering it to be unnecessarily complicated and expensive, and following the successful operation of the McBrayne *Lochiel* favoured the simpler alternative of variable speed engines coupled to a reversing gearbox via a clutch. They were at the time engaged in the design of a vessel employing mechanical transmission to the paddles for their Queensferry service and recommended this system for the new Lymington ferry. However, the Southern Railway officials wanted belt and braces safety when negotiating the Lymington river and insisted on the more expensive diesel-electric drive on the grounds that if one diesel engine failed both paddle wheels could still be driven from one diesel-generator set, albeit at reduced power. The Forth ferries overcame this problem by having the two paddle shafts mechanically connected via a dog-clutch, thus enabling the paddles to be interconnected or independently operated as required, but as completely independent paddle wheels were fitted to the Southern Railway ship the interconnection had to be achieved electrically.

The new vessel, christened *Farringford* by Mrs Biddle, was launched at Dumbarton on 24 March 1947, and with a length of 178 ft, breadth 49ft 6 ins, and gross tonnage of 489 and was the largest ship ever employed on the route. Her capacity was double that of *Lymington* — 32 cars and 320 passengers, or 800 passengers only, — with first and third class lounges and buffets but not much in the way of open deck passenger space. Following a rough weather passage from the Clyde, which took over two weeks, she finally arrived at Southampton on 6 February 1948 and after some repairs gave a demonstration and Press cruise on Friday 27 February in Southampton Water with Captain Woolgar in command. On the return journey the newly converted Red Funnel diesel-electric screw *Vecta* exchanged compliments with the Southern Railway diesel-electric paddler, their sirens trumpeting victory for paddle and screw over the alien Voith Schneider interloper. Insofar as the railway car ferries were concerned, it was to be the one and only victory!

With both *Lymington* and *Farringford* in service during the 1947 season traffic increased dramatically on the Lymington-Yarmouth route. 350,000 passengers were carried, a 60 per cent increase on 1938, and 32,000 motor vehicles, an astounding 600 per cent growth over the 1938 figure. Both vessels coped well in the early post-war years but in 1951, the future of *Lymington* once again came under review.

Plate 65. *Farringford* in latter years with twin masts and exhaust extensions and radar. Her machinery layout was a development of the design used in the pioneer diesel-electric Forth car ferries built by Dennys in 1934. (John Hendy)

CHAPTER 6

NEW PROPS FOR OLD

Captain Goldsworthy continued to maintain his close association with the Southampton marine technical staff and shortly after the nationalisation of the railways on 1 January 1948 paid them a further visit. Nothing had really changed; the Southern Railway had now become Southern Region of the unified British Railways but had lost none of its old individuality and colour. Sir Eustace Missenden, former General Manager of the Southern Railway had been appointed Chairman of the Railway Executive and his previous assistant, John Elliot, to the post of Chief Regional Officer, Southern Region, ensuring that the Southern tradition was maintained under the new regime. Mr Biddle had returned to his former post of Docks & Marine Manager but Mr McQueen had been succeeded as Superintendent Marine Engineer by Mr J.P. Campbell, ably supported by Mr Liston, now designated Marine Engineer, Southampton.

During the early post war years Lymington continued to perform reasonably well, although the costs involved in constantly changing and repairing the propellers were acceptable solely on account of her being the only ship able to maintain the service in severe weather. The solution to the propeller problems continued to elude the technical experts, although Voith themselves held the opinion that the ship was being called upon to operate in conditions totally unsuitable for Voith Schneider propellers. They advocated transferring her to an alternative route where she would not be required to run in a narrow, shallow channel. However, it is very difficult to reconcile this view, and the problems experienced with Lymington when considering the case of the Katsena, which for ten years had ploughed her way through the mud, debris and flotsam of a river in darkest Africa without serious trouble, whereas one in service on the bustling civilised waters of the Solent had been plagued with continual breakdowns. Neither shortening the propeller blades, nor fitting a variety of protecting skegs had made any noticeable difference — other than to reduce her speed — and there was no predictable pattern to the timing of propeller failures. Breakdowns sometimes occured only a few hours after being put back into service following an overhaul, with no indication as to the cause. It was felt instinctively that the angle at which the propellers were mounted was responsible, but why? . . . .why? . . . .why?

At a meeting held in Southampton on 1 July 1948 Captain Goldsworthy urged Mr Campbell to seriously consider removing the propellers and remounting them vertically, since no other vessel had suffered the perpetual problems experienced with Lymington. This time, however, he went further and suggested the drastic step of mounting both propellers at the stern and converting her to single ended operation. There was some logic behind this, since both propellers would be well protected from damage and in addition the best efficiency was obtained with a single ended vessel, but Mr Campbell quickly swept aside any thoughts of a single ended Lymington with the comment:

"Regarding the possibility of carrying out the extensive alterations to Lymington which you suggest, our best feature on this vessel is the wonderful manoeuvrability owing to having propellers at both ends. If we altered this I do not think she would be of much interest to us, since in heavy cross winds in the Lymington river she is the only ship which can carry on the service."

And there, for the time being, the matter was allowed to rest.

Plate 66. Lymington after fitting of radar. Note the painting of the wheelhouse brown, a new feature after strengthening to take the radar mast. If registrations are to be trusted, then the returning holidaymakers in the first car have all the way back to Walsall to drive. (Fraser MacHaffie)

Salt Water Cooling

Apart from the propellers Lymington's troubles had been very few and far between. The Allen main engines proved to be robust, simple to maintain and required little attention other than routine maintenance in spite of being cooled by salt water, circulated by means of a constant speed electrical impeller type vertical pump and without any form of thermostatic temperature control. The full flow was thus maintained regardless of engine loading, although the incoming water could be diverted by means of a manually operated by-pass valve if required. The Clyde diesel-electric paddler Talisman, also salt water cooled, had her four main engine cylinder blocks replaced twice within five years on account of cracks developing in the blocks, and was then converted to fresh water cooling. Although her engines were of a difficult make the choice of salt water cooling for Lymington seemed to be a recipe for certain disaster, and although some trouble was experienced, Lymington still retains her salt water cooling to this day. The cooling water is taken from port or starboard inlets (both if the ship is rolling badly) via a strainer plate and then through a coconut matting filter before being pumped through the main engine oil coolers, cylinder blocks and heads. The filter, which trapped the mud and silt drawn in with the river water, had to be frequently removed and washed out, although inevitably some of the mud did get carried through to the engines. The first sign of a build up of sludge in the engines themselves was a decrease in lubricating oil pressure due to the oil cooler becoming silted up, which then had to be cleaned and the cylinder blocks hosed out to clear the sludge which had settled in the base. In the late 'forties the top seating of one of the cylinder liners corroded away and had to be repaired by boring out the top of the block and a false ring fitted, but unfortunately this proved to be merely the first in a sequence and was followed by others cracking and crumbling away. A pair of replacement cylinder blocks was supplied by Allen's in April 1950 and these are still in service. The usual operating practice on the Solent was to keep the engines running at reduced speed if the vessel was stopped for less than half an hour and to shut down only when the stop exceeded this time. As a matter of interest Fishbourne, Wootton and Hilsea were all salt water cooled and gave no trouble in this respect.

More discussions

Lymington struck another bad patch in the summer of 1952 when breakdowns occured during busy weekends and traffic had to be diverted, with great inconvenience to all concerned, to the Portsmouth-Fishbourne service. Towards the end of January 1953 *Lymington* again blotted her copybook when one propeller failed and she had to be taken out of service, since the spare was being overhauled at the time. This intensified the complaints from Isle of Wight interests seriously concerned with the inadequacy of the Lymington-Yarmouth services and who were pressing for an Air Car Ferry Service. Although British Railways opposed this scheme, and contended they provided an adequate service by water, the unreliability of *Lymington* and consequent interruptions to the service was widely quoted in support of the Air Ferry proposal. *Lymington* was kept sailing for as long as possible between propeller changes even though oil losses under such circumstances were very high. At times she was losing oil from the propellers at the rate of a barrel (40 gallons) per round trip and barrels were stacked at the top of the Lymington slipway so as to be readily available.

With the continual increase of traffic on the route, and the ill-will resulting from the frequent interruptions to the service the management decided some positive action had to be taken and following a meeting at Southampton Captain Goldsworthy wrote to Voith almost in despair. The conversion of *Vecta* to normal twin-screw propulsion had been well publicised in the local and technical press, which had done nothing for the image of the Voith Schneider propeller in this country, and whenever Captain Goldsworthy attempted to interest shipowners in Voith Schneider propulsion a not unusual response would be: "What about *Vecta* then?" In his eyes it was vital to prevent *Lymington* being converted to other means of propulsion, since a second abandonment would have sounded the death knell for the Voith Schneider propeller in this country, or at the least made it very difficult to secure any further business. The simplest, least expensive and most attractive alternative would be to remount the propellers vertically, but the management were still hesitant about committing themselves to such a heavy outlay when a successful outcome was still uncertain. Voith in their reply to Captain Goldsworthy's letter, advised that in their opinion the best solution would be not only to remount the propellers vertically, but also to replace them with those of the latest design. A price was given for three new units and during the summer the railway marine staff carefully considered all the options open to them and then, on 20 August 1953, invited Captain Goldsworthy to attend a meeting at Southampton when the future of *Lymington* was to be discussed. The importance of the occasion can be judged from the fact that it was the first time the subject of *Lymington's* performance was to be discussed directly with the Docks & Marine Manager, all of Captain Goldsworthy's previous meetings having been with the technical staff only. In the event Mr Biddle was unable to attend the meeting, and in his absence the chair was taken by his assistant, Mr Isaac, who opened by outlining the frequent stoppages of the service which caused great inconvenience to, and many complaints from, passengers travelling to and from the Isle of Wight via Lymington. He then stated the measures which would now have to be taken to provide a reliable service and satisfy the public, and enumerated the courses available to achieve this:

1) Improvements to the *Lymington's* Voith Schneider propellers.
2) Conversion of *Lymington* to double twin-screw.
3) Scrap *Lymington* and build a new ship.

It is interesting to note that a conversion to paddle propulsion was not even mentioned.

Most of the discussion centred on proposal No. 1, since both Mr Campbell and Mr Liston were anxious to retain the Voith Schneider system but to elimate the breakdowns. They pointed out that the Lymington river was now no longer filled with baulks of timber and had also been dredged to a greater width, whilst in addition there had been no indication for a long time of the propeller blades having received heavy blows or suffered the effects of deep dredging in gravel. The overall width between the outboard blade orbits of *Lymington* was a mere 27ft., compared with the 49ft., between the ends of the paddle floats of *Farringford*, which sailed at all states of the tide without damage. There must therefore be some other reason why *Lymington's* propellers were subject to so many failures when other vessels similarly equipped were perfectly satisfactory, and they had come to the conclusion that this must be due to the angle at which the propellers were mounted having an adverse effect on the blade shaft needle bearings. The sequence appeared to be that the uncaged needles first of all jammed and broke up, causing vibration, seal failure, welding fractures and entry of water. (In this they were absolutely correct, although the reason *why* the needle rollers broke up still required explanation). What they ideally required, therefore, was to modify *Lymington* so that the propellers could be vertically mounted in such a position that the top of the unit was

above the water line so that a propeller could be changed with the vessel afloat instead of having to go into a slipway or mud bank. As it was, changing a propeller normally took 24 hours, or even 36 hours if tidal conditions were unfavourable, hence the desire to be able to change a propeller with the vessel afloat.

In response to a request by Captain Goldsworthy prior to the meeting Voith had prepared two schemes whereby the propellers could be mounted vertically or almost so, but the first was discounted since it only reduced the propeller angle from 22½° to about 9° an inclination still considered unacceptable by the Southampton men. The second was rather more novel, and proposed fitting two small fore and aft sponsons on which the propellers would be vertically mounted and with the tops above the water, but as this would place them even further outboard than at present and thus susceptible to damage when berthing and in heavy seas this scheme was also rejected. The question of altering *Lymington* to single ended construction was again raised and again discarded, since the owners were quite adamant that double ended construction was essential in order to avoid having to turn in the river, particularly as it was intended to replace the *PS Freshwater* with a further double ended vessel in the near future. At present, a wide pool had to be kept dredged to enable *Freshwater* to turn off the pier, an expense the company wished to eliminate. The meeting ended with Captain Goldsworthy being asked to request Voith for further proposals which would meet the owners' requirements.

Voith responded with a third variation whereby the propellers were moved further forward but kept within the run of the hull by mounting them vertically on an appendage welded to the underside of the hull. They again stressed that as the existing propellers must inevitably have suffered some slight distortions on account of the numerous repairs effected it would be wise to fit new propellers of the latest type, which had only four blades and incorporated a new design of kinematics, resulting in fewer and more robust working parts. A price of £14,244 was quoted for three propellers of this type. This was certainly the most practical solution to the problem, but the niggling doubt still remained — would the recommended alterations eliminate the propeller failures? As no-one would give an unequivocal affirmative to this question Mr Biddle still hesitated over recommending to the Board a substantial expenditure on alterations and new propellers, although the general consensus was that they should take the plunge. *Lymington* herself, no doubt fed up with the constant procrastination, finally prodded Mr Biddle into a decision by breaking down in mid-February 1954, when *Farringford* happened to be undergoing annual overhaul. The Southern Region was experiencing a rather unhappy spell at the time; a strike had halted the Island railway services and now the west Wight crossing had to be suspended, with Lymington-Yarmouth passengers having to travel via Southampton-Cowes and then by bus to Yarmouth, an inconvenience not calculated to endear British Railways to their long suffering Isle of Wight travellers. Mr Biddle had the doubtful pleasure of having to face deputations of disgruntled residents, and tried to mollify the irate deputees by informing them he now hoped modifications designed to eliminate the problems experienced with *Lymington* would be carried out and that in the meantime he would make every effort to provide a satisfactory service for them. He was as good as his word, and approval for the necessary alterations to *Lymington* and the purchase of three new propellers was given in mid-March. Mr Biddle informed Captain Goldsworthy of the decision

to go ahead with the conversion and then added ominously:

"If this doesn't work I'll get shot, but I'll shoot you first!"

In order to see what could be done to avoid any breakdowns during the forthcoming summer season Voith sent across their chief erector, Herr Buhr — Schubert had now retired — and a further meeting took place at Southampton, this time chaired by Mr Biddle himself, whose attitude was described as "friendly, but fed up!" He said he felt they were suffering from being the pioneers of Voith Schneider propulsion in this country and explained the bad feeling engendered by the frequent breakdowns of *Lymington*. They had made the decision to modify the vessel and he had high hopes that the new vertically mounted propellers would provide the answer to their difficulties, but as these would not be delivered for some 10 months his immediate problem was to keep the ship in service during this period. The problems experienced were carefully explained to Herr Buhr with the request that any help Voith or Herr Buhr could give would be greatly appreciated. In fact, nothing could really be done except to hope and pray!

Lymington, perhaps sensing she was at last to be rid of her life-long affliction responded to the prayers by behaving herself, with only a minor hiccup or two, until withdrawn for the propeller transplant during the 1954/55 winter.

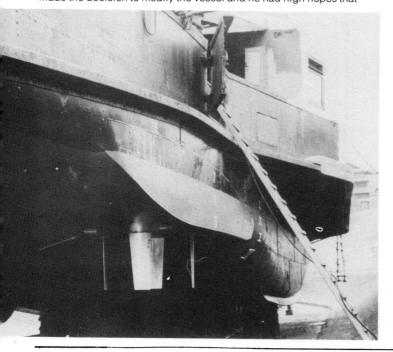

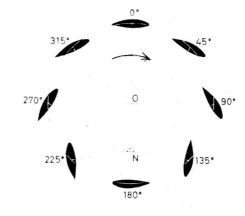

Plate 68. New vertically mounted propeller and hull blister. (E.C. Goldsworthy & Co.)

Plate 67. (opposite page). The success of the new propellers resulted in a new VSP ship for the Lymington service. Here the pioneer is framed from the bow ramp of the *Freshwater* which is about to embark the dignitaries on the pier for her inaugural cruise. (Alan Brown collection)

Figure 12. Flip from head-out to head-in position.

A successful operation

The complete transplant operation, including the hull and drive-shaft modifications, was carried out at Southampton, and the installation of the new propellers supervised by the Voith 'consultant', Herr Buhr. The latter were located further forward than the originals, and the drive shaft had to be lengthened by means of a cardan shaft in order to vary the direction in both the horizontal and vertical planes, a most unusual feature for a British ship but quite common on the continental vessels. The protection skegs were also removed since these caused additional drag and had reduced the speed. The propellers arrived at Southampton in February 1955, and by 1 April one propeller was in place and being lined up. Trials were run in May, when *Lymington* attained a speed of just under 9 knots during blustery weather and with squalls reaching force 8-9. This rather disappointing result was partly due to the lack of stabilising skegs, which resulted in poor course keeping and hence reduced the forward thrust, although the owners appeared to be quite satisfied with this speed. She returned to service in early May and spent a trouble-free summer on the route, to the delight of all concerned. Captain Wilkins, her regular master, wrote to Captain Goldsworthy on 15 August and commented:

"The recently fitted propellers on *Lymington* are a complete success."

and on 5 October Mr Campbell added to the praise:

"The propellers have now been running satisfactorily for approximately 1200 hours, including idling time at the berth, and it is not proposed to interfere with them in any way during the refit period".

Perhaps the most pleasing comment, however, was contained in a letter written by Mr Biddle on 5 July to Captain Goldsworthy:

"You will be pleased to know that the vessel is operating very successfully . . . . arising from this, we have under consideration building a new ship for the service with similar propellers."

The Lymington services manager, Mr Morford, was also delighted with his reformed problem child, and several years later neatly summed up the complete transformation that had taken place with the following comment:

"When she finally went into service with the new propellers she ran for 2½ years without incident. One propeller was then lifted out solely because the engineering officials at head-quarters were curious to see what signs of wear (if any) were visible. The result — practically nil. Never was money better spent — these propellers had already paid for themselves and were to do so in future over and over again."

Diagnosis

Lymington's first 18 years could scarcely be described as successful but it would be equally misleading to regard her as a failure since she had convinced her owners that no other propulsion method could remotely approach the Voith Schneider for manoeuvrability, ease of handling and general convenience. Indeed there were times when *Lymington* had been the only vessel capable of making the passage, solely on account of her skipper being able to retain control under the most adverse conditions, and this characteristic had been one of her saving graces. So, with the benefit of 50 years experience and hindsight just what was the cause of *Lymington's* propeller problems? The fundamental error undoubtedly lay in mounting the propellers at an angle of 22½° outboard from the vertical; what is not quite so easy to see is why. In fairness to Denny's it should be made clear that Voith's insistence on the propellers being vertically mounted was based more on intuition and a fear of mechanical damage than to any precise knowledge as to why this was so vitally necessary. It was because of this lack of understanding by all parties that the mechanical damage red herring was pursued for so long. Although dredging through gravel and sand undoubtedly added to the propeller stresses it was not in itself the basic cause of the failures, and even when the propeller transplant was made no one was prepared to give a hard and fast guarantee on a successful outcome, simply because at that time the real reasons for the failures were still unidentified.

As so often is the case, no single cause was responsible; in this instance design, lubrication and operation factors combined to produce disastrous effects in an inclined propeller though not in one vertically mounted. The Germans were all for 'efficiency', and to this end uncaged needle roller bearings rather than plain bushes were used to support the blade shafts in the pots. These bearings were lubricated by the general flow of oil in the propeller, with the rapid movement of each blade as it swung from the 'head at' to the 'head in (see fig. 12) creating a pumping action through the shaft bearings, thus continually renewing the oil film. Whilst this worked perfectly satisfactorily in the case of a vertically mounted propeller the additional bearing load due to the weight of an angled blade was probably quite sufficient to cancel this pumping action, in which case the oil film was not being replaced with fresh oil and consequently overheated and disintegrated. As a result the bearing ran dry and the needles jammed and broke, setting up vibrations which destroyed the blade shaft seals and fractured the shaft bearing pots. Eventually water, sand and silt were drawn in, compounding the damage and the propeller had to be changed. Paradoxically, the situation was probably aggravated by the very quick flip of the blade from the head-out to the head-in position. With inclined propellers the flip position would be at the highest point on one propeller and the lowest on the other when running straight ahead and although the exact position at which it occured was not

particularly important, what did matter was that the flip would be augmented by the weight of the blade in one direction and reduced in the other. This enhanced flip could cause jarring of the needles and thus intensify the stresses on the already shaky bearing.

The use of uncaged needle roller bearings was eventually superseded by caged needles and then by plain bushes, although in some of the latest high output propellers roller bearings have been found to be necessary. Unfortunately, none of these design changes came in time to benefit *Lymington* but in any case may have done little more than alleviate the problem. If only the propellers had been mounted correctly when the vessel was being built there seems little doubt she would have been completely satisfactory. Denny's compromise had been a very expensive piece of fudge indeed!

Plate 69. *Freshwater* at Fishbourne. In size she was slightly smaller than *Farringford*. (R. Butcher)

A new lease of life

If *Lymington's* first 18 years had been more than a little turbulent, the following 18 were quite the reverse. The new vertically mounted propellers justified all the predictions made and confidence expressed in them and *Lymington*, together with *Farringford*, now maintained a reliable and regular service. In 1955, *Lymington's* first full year with the new propellers, a total of 7904 commercial vehicles, 41,911 cars, 6,646 motor cycles and — a reminder of a now vanished form of transport — 1282 motor cycle combinations were conveyed, together with 623,266 passengers. Within a further three years it had become quite obvious that the two car ferries could not satisfactorily cope with the ever-rising demand for motor vehicle accommodation on the route and it was decided to replace the passenger only paddle steamer *Freshwater* with a new passenger/car ferry in 1959. This time there was no hesitation or argument over what type of propulsion system to specify and Mr Biddle's comment to Captain Goldsworthy in 1955, that the company had under consideration the building of a new ship for the service with Voith Schneider propellers, at last became a reality in 1959. Built by the Ailsa Shipbuilding Co. Ltd., Troon, and christened *Freshwater*, the new ship made her maiden voyage on 21 September 1959. With a length of 164ft and 42ft beam she was slightly smaller than the ungainly looking *Farringford*, and with a capacity of 620 passengers and 26 cars could be described as an improved and enlarged version of *Lymington*. The Voith Schneider propellers were driven by a pair of 8 cylinder Crossley two-stroke diesel engines, giving a speed of 10.5 knots. Promenade decks having permanent deck seating for 200 passengers were a welcome return after the Farringford's lack of open air accommodation since the Voith Schneider layout permitted side and under deck passenger saloons

to be provided and hence more open deck space. Following *Freshwater's* entry into service *Lymington* was demoted to spare and relief vessel although the volume of traffic ensured her full employment during the busy summer months, when all three vessels were required.

Until the mid-sixties livestock was carried 'on the hoof' and it was not unusual for *Lymington* to make a special 'cattle only' trip once a week. Sometimes the car deck would be completely packed with sheep, making it impossible to get either into or out of the saloons or engine room. Eventually, after an accident when one animal broke its leg coming up the ramp and had to be destroyed by the RSPCA on the spot, in full view of the passengers, it was decided that in future livestock would be conveyed in cattle lorries only. In addition, loading large quantities of livestock often caused lengthly delays, resulting in missed rail or bus connection, and the use of cattle transporters effected a great improvement in this respect. Circuses, too, were quite a problem, and had to be transported in sections — sometimes on special night sailings — in order to avoid delays to the normal services.

The Yarmouth Harbour Commissioners, in their 1961 Annual Report announced a record number of passengers carried that year, with *Freshwater* and *Farringford* maintaining the scheduled services supplemented by *Lymington* as and when necessary. In addition 7,000 more cars had been carried than in any previous year and as priority had to be given to passengers this reduced the number of cars which could be carried on runs with heavy passenger loadings. This resulted in many complaints from motorists who found it difficult to understand why a vessel with a half empty car deck was said to be fully booked — perhaps a Board of Trade official should have been stationed at the pier to explain their regulations to irate motorists! Indeed, such was the growth in passenger traffic on the route that the manager, Mr Robins, predicted that in future the Lymington-Yarmouth service would come to be regarded more as a passenger route than a car ferry passage — a rather surprising statement to make at the beginning of the car-mad era.

During the 'sixties *Lymington* came to be increasingly used on the Portsmouth-Fishbourne service to cover overhaul periods and breakdowns of the regular vessels. From the records which I have been able to consult it appears that the first of these was on Saturday 11 August 1962 when *Fishbourne* damaged a propeller and had to go to Southampton for repairs. *Lymington* was accordingly despatched to Portsmouth with a Lymington crew and then crossed light to Fishbourne to load. *Camber Queen* and *Lymington* continued to operate the service until the traffic was finally cleared in the early hours of Sunday. *Lymington* was again on the run on Monday until withdrawn at 12.45pm, following the reinstatement of *Fishbourne* at 12 noon, and then returned to Lymington. She was back at Portsmouth on Tuesday 18th September, when *Camber Queen* suffered port engine failure and put in a couple of evening runs before returning to Lymington. Just twelve months later *Lymington* was again required at Portsmouth, this time to cover for *Fishbourne*, which had to be withdrawn for some minor repairs, and did two runs to the island. From January 1964 *Lymington* officially acted as stand-by vessel on both routes and spent most of January, February and March at Portsmouth prior to going for survey at the beginning of April. This year (1964) proved to be an exceptionally interesting one for the Lymington ships for both *Freshwater* and *Farringford* underwent trials on a route not normally associated with car ferries. *Freshwater* sailed to Ryde on Monday 21 September for gangway tests at No's 2 and 3 berths and then proceeded to Portsmouth where similar tests were carried out at the south end of the Harbour pier. A month later, on the morning of 19 October, *Farringford* crossed from Lymington to Ryde Pier, where she was met by a bevy of local and headquarters (London) officials. After berthing and gangway tests had been carried out under their watchful eyes *Farringford*, now with her VIP observers on board, first proceeded to Fishbourne and then paddled across the Solent to the Camber. Here, Captain Dove, the Chief Marine Superintendent (Victoria) insisted on personally taking the vessel onto the slipway, an operation requiring a couple of 90° turns. Captain Dove showed he had lost none of his handling skills and aided by *Farringford's* independent paddle wheels completed the manoeuvre without difficulty. *Farringford* also

extricated herself from this awkward spot quite easily and then continued to the harbour pier for gangway trials. All tests were carried out to the satisfaction of the officials and *Farringford* returned to Lymington covered in glory.

Lymington paid her first 1965 visit to Portsmouth on 11 March, when it was intended to put her on the run the following day, but the service had to be cancelled since she managed to get a rope wound round one of her propellers and had to return to the hulk. The rope was cleared by a diver on the 15th (Saturday) but as propeller repairs were also required it was not until the 19th that she was able to make a trial run to Fishbourne and back. A further trial run was made on the evening of the 26th and after a single round trip on the 30th and again on 2nd April she returned to Lymington on the 5th. She was back at Southampton on 21 April for annual survey and following completion again entered service on the 21st May on the Portsmouth-Fishbourne route. All went well until the 28th, when she grounded on the Fishbourne slipway at 13.10 and defied all attempts to free her. She stuck there until 20.19, completely blocking access to other vessels until 20.25 when she finally managed to get away. To clear the back-log of traffic she ran two round trips from Portsmouth, finishing her unscheduled sailings at 00.55 hours. None the worse for her trip ashore and night out she was back on the run later in the morning and then returned to Lymington in the evening.

In March 1965 work commenced on an extension of the Yarmouth slipway to permit easier berthing of the ferries at low water periods. The work was carried out in two stages, dealing with one half of the width of the slipway at a time in order to avoid interruption of the ferry service and using temporary pontoons to keep the vessel in position.

An outstanding innovation in 1962 was the introduction of an experimental service on peak Friday nights between Portsmouth and Fishbourne, with departures at midnight, 02.00, 04.00 and 06.00 hours from the mainland and the odd hours from the island. This service became a regular feature and, in addition, an extra vessel was transferred from Lymington when necessary to relieve congestion on Saturday nights, with *Lymington* being used on both these services from time to time.

For example, she was on the overnight Fishbourne runs on 23/24 August 1965, and 22/23 July 1966, but the most interesting event took place on 27 March 1967, when, after operating the Portsmouth-Fishbourne service in the morning she transferred to the **Portsmouth Harbour-Ryde** route in the afternoon. After making four

Plate 70. After the entry into service of *Freshwater*, *Lymington* still covered as spare and relief vessel. In this Yarmouth shot the increasing congestion caused by motor traffic awaiting the crossing at peak times can be seen. (Fraser MacHaffie)

Plate 71. *Freshwater* with new masts and in 'monastral' blue livery with 'barbed wire' device approaching Yarmouth. (T. Cooper)

round trips she returned to the Fishbourne service in the evening. The relevant page from the deck log is to be included and so far as can be ascertained this was the only occasion which she was employed on the Portsmouth passenger-only service. (see appendix 4).

The electrification of the London-Bournemouth route in 1967, including the branch from Brockenhurst (on the main line) to Lymington Pier, when a basic hourly service was introduced cut the London-Lymington journey time by 40 minutes and resulted in a marked increase in passenger traffic. Well over half the passengers carried on the British Rail ferry services between the mainland and Isle of Wight that year travelled by the Lymington-Yarmouth route — 878,129 out of a total of 1,339,658. In addition 109,135 cars and 7,013 commercial vehicles, including coaches, used the service in comparison with 273,556 and 24,044 on the Fishbourne service and to cope with this increase in traffic an all-night service was introduced, which carried a full complement of cars on most crossings. By 1968 demands made upon the service necessitated improvements to both terminals, and at Lymington a £30,000 scheme officially opened in August included the construction of a new terminal building housing a booking office, staff accommodation, catering facilities and stores together with an enlarged car parking area. At Yarmouth a new booking hall and improved car parking were provided. At the same time a novel role for *Lymington* was proposed by the Isle of Wight Services manager, who announced that he would like two new ferries for the Lymington-Yarmouth route and *Lymington* to inaugurate a Portsmouth-Gosport service. He was to get his two new Lymington ferries eventually, but nothing further was ever heard of the Gosport scheme. The service was severely disrupted on 10 August in the same year when *Freshwater* became stranded on the Yarmouth slipway due to an unusually rapid falling tide and although the 30 cars and 100 passengers she had on board for the 04.05 crossing were disembarked to try and free her she remained firmly attached to terra-firma. *Farringford,* meanwhile had left Lymington at 04.00 and landed her passengers at Yarmouth Pier, but the unfortunate motorists had to wait until 09.15 when the rising tide freed *Freshwater.*

In spite of a slight drop in car traffic in 1969 British Rail stated its intention of increasing the capacity of the two larger ferries on the Lymington-Yarmouth run, and, to use Captain Wheeler's own words "the third ferry, the old *Lymington* was to be overhauled, made more habitable, and used to carry passengers only to Yarmouth pier." It was also announced that two new larger vessels were under consideration in order to increase the capacity on the route, and that it was intended for these to be introduced in 1971/72. The planned refurbishing of *Lymington* was carried out during her overhaul and survey in the winter of 1969/70. Some relaying of the top deck planking had been done in October, and in February 1970 she went to Husband's at Marchwood for the hull to be shot blasted and replated as necessary. Steel plates were also fitted over the engine room and one of the original Ruston generators replaced by a larger Ruston set obtained second-hand from one of the Dover train ferries. A new d.c. motor driven alternator enabled fluorescent strip lighting to be installed in the passenger accommodation, where the original grey-green moquette upholstery was replaced with plain green vinyl. In spite of Captain Wheeler's predictions 'the old *Lymington'* retained her car-carrying capacity and continued to be used as much for the remainder of her time on the Solent.

An hourly Monday to Friday service was introduced in the 1969/70 winter timetable instead of two-hourly as previously and in March 1971 a £30,000 dredging scheme to widen the main channel near Pylewell Lake from 120 feet to 250 feet over a length of 900 feet was announced. The object was to enable the ferries to pass in the river instead of only in the Solent, and thus permit a half-hourly service to be run on peak weekends. A contract for this work to be done had actually been placed in February, with a completion date of 1 April, but owing to problems with equipment the dredging was not finished until later in the year.

In the spring of 1972 British Rail announced their intention to replace *Lymington* and *Farringford* with two new ferries similar to the *Cuthred,* which had entered service on the Portsmouth-Fishbourne service in 1969. The new vessels were ordered from Robb Caledon Shipbuilders, Dundee, and with dimensions of 750 tons gross, 192 feet in length and 51 feet beam marked a further increase in size for ferries on the western route. Maximum capacity was increased to 750 passengers and 52 cars, although the latter dropped if coaches or lorries were carried. Propulsion was by Voith Schneider propellers giving a speed of 10 knots. The first of the pair, christened *Cenwulf,* entered service on 18 October 1973 and was joined by her sister *Cenred,* early in the new year.

Farringford made her final service runs on 8 November, and in January was towed to Hull for conversion to side loading, where she replaced the *PS Wingfield Castle* on the Hull-New Holland ferry service. *Lymington's* last service runs were made on the following day, the 9th, after which she sailed to Portsmouth, was advertised for sale, and laid up in Portchester lake awaiting a purchaser. She had spent 36 years on the ferry run, not a bad life's work on an arduous, all year round, all weather service, and was still in remarkably sound and solid condition.

Her retirement was to be of very brief duration.

Plate 72. An aerial view of Yarmouth with Cosen's *Embassy* at the pier, *Freshwater* approaching and *Lymington* receding. (Alan Brown collection)

Plate 73. It's not all happy Summer Saturdays! Chief Engineer Fred Howland glumly surveys a wintery outlook at Lymington during the 1963/64 winter. (Fred Howland).

Plate 74. (Below). *Lymington* at the hulk at Portsmouth. She is still in the old colours whilst *Camber Queen* and *Shanklin,* both recently overhauled, sport the new 1965 colour scheme. (R.Silsbury)

Plate 75. 'Up the Creek'. *Lymington* in new livery approaches Lymington slipway. (Fraser MacHaffie)

Plate 76. (Below). *Lymington* unloading at Lymington in her latter years. Now in BR blue livery at least a white strake between the boot topping and the blue has been added. (Fraser MacHaffie)

CHAPTER 7

NORTH OF THE BORDER

A number of offers were received for *Lymington* during the 1973/74 winter, the most serious of these being from Western Ferries (Argyll) Ltd., the private enterprise vehicle ferry operator with routes in the West Highlands and Firth of Clyde. Although the Voith Schneider propeller was entirely new to them (the two vessels currently employed on the Firth of Clyde crossing were double single screw i.e., a single screw at each end) they were desperately in need of an extra vessel to cover breakdowns, maintenance work and survey periods on their two ship service. *Lymington* had come onto the market at exactly the right time and the deal was finally clinched in March 1974.

Plate 77. Cars disembarking at Lamlash from the after deck of the LMS turbine steamer *Glen Sannox.* This operation was only possible when the tides were suitable. (G.E.Langmuir)

Clyde Steamer Services

Prior to the latter part of the 19th century steamboat services on the Clyde were provided by a number of relatively small private companies and even single vessels owned and operated by their captains. A great many of these were based at Glasgow but following the establishment of railheads at points along the shores of the firth the railway companies themselves, either directly or through subsidiaries, commenced to operate steamer services from their own coastal rail/ship terminals. The most important were at Craigendoran, (North British Railway) opened in 1882, (although the company had operated out of Helensburgh in 1866 and from 1869 onwards), Princes Pier, Greenock (Glasgow & South Western Railway) used from 1891 and Gourock (Caledonian Railway) in 1889. On the lower firth railheads were established at Wemyss Bay (Caledonian), Fairlie (Glasgow & South Western), and Ardrossan Harbour (Caledonian and Glasgow & South Western), and by the outbreak of war in 1914 the majority of the Clyde coast passenger traffic was concentrated in the hands of the railway owned fleets. General goods were handled by small privately owned cargo vessels and "puffers" — small coasters capable of unloading at primitive piers or direct on to the beach and specialising in handling bulk cargoes such as coal, stone, timber and similar materials. The situation changed little after the amalgamation of the railways in 1923, when the London Midland and Scottish Railway took over the Caledonian and Glasgow & South Western systems and the North British became part of the London & North Eastern Railway. As a result the LMSR became the dominant passenger steamship owner on the Clyde, operating out of Greenock, Gourock, Wemyss Bay, Fairlie and Ardrossan, all situated on the southern shore of the firth. The sole north bank terminal, Craigendoran, and the former North British fleet came under the control of the LNER.

Between the wars few cars were transported across the firth or to the islands, and in those days this meagre traffic was mainly conveyed by the passenger steamers. When the tide happened to be suitable cars were run over a couple of stout wooden planks from the pier onto the promenade deck of the paddle steamers and parked on the space around the funnel or, in the case of the turbines, on the after deck. Indeed, one of the reasons for the popularity of the islands as family resorts, particularly by Glaswegians, was the virtually traffic-free roads, and Bute even boasted its own tramway system until 1936. Another popular, but perhaps more cosmopolitan, watering place was Dunoon and its satellites on the Cowal coast.

Although actually on the mainland a long and circuitous journey over narrow, hilly and winding roads was necessary to reach Dunoon from industrial Clydeside and by far the quickest and most convenient route was via rail to either Craigendoran or Gourock and thence by steamer. In spite of the road access, albeit inconvenient, the heaviest Firth of Clyde car traffic was carried on the Gourock-Dunoon passage and in the late 'thirties some 1000 cars were being conveyed annually by the railway steamers on this run. Prodded by the Ministry of Transport — ever road biased — and with the success of the Southern Railway's Isle of Wight services as an example of how it could be done, the LMSR tentatively investigated the possibility of a car ferry service between Gourock and Dunoon. Although details of their deliberations on the subject are sparse, there were in fact a number of options which the company considered. The fundamental question, of course, was whether to inaugurate a separate vehicle only (with occupants) route or to incorporate the new scheme into the existing Gourock-Dunoon service. In the case of the former a shorter crossing was feasible, and "The Motor" reported that the LMSR had under consideration a car ferry service from Cloch Point to Dunoon. No doubt the simplest scheme for a pure car ferry would have been to construct unsophisticated end-loading terminals at these points, and it is interesting, in view of later developments, that the LMSR did consider this option, although Parliamentary approval would have been necessary for them to operate such a service. However, the volume of traffic scarcely warranted an independent car ferry service, although this would undoubtedly have increased with the improved facilities. The use of a double-ended passenger/vehicle ferry on the recognised route between Gourock and Dunoon was thus a more attractive proposition, provided that the new slipways could be arranged to take advantage of the existing terminal facilities as, for example, the Southern Railway had done at Lymington. A third possibility, since rail and foot passengers constituted the bulk of the traffic, would be to use the existing piers and provide a hoist either on the piers or on the ship itself to enable embarkation of cars at all states of the tide. Although such a scheme necessitated the side loading of vehicles this was not deemed to be any disadvantage; indeed, side loading from either slipways or pontoons was used on the Tay, Forth, Humber, Thames, Severn and other car ferries at that time. The utilisation of a platform hoist or vertically movable deck on a ship was not an entirely novel idea since this method was in fact employed on some of the Clyde Navigation Trust's vehicle ferries crossing the upper reaches of the River Clyde. The advantage of having the hoist on the ship meant that no part of the pier was restricted to the vehicle ferries only, and the latter would be able to use other piers in emergencies. All these options were seriously examined by the LMSR, but it is believed that the vehicle hoist system was viewed with the greatest favour and that enquiries were made concerning the design of a suitable vessel. However, the outbreak of war halted progress before any definite decision had been made, and the scheme was shelved "for the duration".

In the immediate post-war years the Clyde rail and steamer services continued in much the same manner as formerly, although with a much depleted fleet in the case of the LMSR. Several of the

paddle steamers had been lost on active service, or were deemed to be not worthy of reconditioning after their war-time duties, and the threatened nationalisation of the railways inhibited any serious steps being taken to rehabilitate the fleet. This threat became a reality on 1 January 1948 when the railways, together with their associated shipping interests, amalgamated under the blanket ownership of the British Transport Commission and were controlled by the Railway Executive. The ex-LMSR and LNER interests in Scotland became the Scottish Region of British Railways, the title adopted for trading purposes. The Caledonian Steam Packet Co. Ltd., was now a subsidiary of the BTC and the ex-LMSR ships continued to be registered in the name of this subsidiary whilst the ex-LNER vessels came under the direct ownership of the BTC until transferred to the CSP in October 1951.

Plate 78. Cars stowed on the after deck of the *Glen Sannox* on passage.   (G.E.Langmuir)

Clyde Car Ferries

The first true vehicle ferries on the firth appeared in July 1951. In that year the privately owned Bute Ferry Company introduced a service between Colintraive and Rhubodach, a point where the island was separated from the mainland by a narrow strip of sheltered water, using small war-time bow loading landing craft on the 5 minute crossing. In spite of the circuitous road journey a direct Glasgow-Bute door-to-door van and lorry service now became possible and the effect was immediate, with the cargo steamers losing a considerable amount of traffic to road transport. At the same time a more ambitious car ferry service between Greenock and Sandbank, a village on the shore of the Holy Loch some 2 miles from Dunoon was planned by Mr John Hall. Ex-naval bow loading tank landing craft, similar to those employed by the same owner on his ill-fated Granton-Burntisland Forth ferry service in 1951, were to be used, but lack of finance and other problems caused the scheme to be abandoned. In the meantime the BTC had been taking a long hard look at the ever-increasing losses sustained by its Clyde steamer operations and in February 1951 the chairman, Lord Hurcomb, announced that a decision had been taken to modernise and reorganise these services. Seven new motor ships were to replace the older coal fired passenger steamers and cargo ships, four of which would be small passenger-only vessels and the remaining three general-purpose craft capable of carrying passengers, motor vehicles, cargo and livestock on the Arran, Bute and Cowal (Dunoon) services. To expect three ships to cover three all-year round routes seemed to be a decidedly optimistic assessment! The 1939 car-ferry proposals had been taken out of their pigeon holes, and after a review of the options it was agreed that the new general purpose vessels had to be capable of loading motor vehicles at all states of the tide from the existing piers. Denny's were given the job of preparing a design and produced a neat, purposeful looking vessel having the passenger accommodation forward and an electrically operated car hoist abaft the funnel leading to a 26 car capacity

garage on the main deck forward of the hoist. A hatch in the promenade deck behind the hoist gave access to a 50 ton capacity hold for general freight and livestock. Two samson posts (quickly christened "goalposts") equipped with derricks were provided to lift containers and loads too heavy for the hoist, and in addition enabled motor vehicles to be unloaded if a hoist failed. In the event, these were very little used, and their removal in the winter of 1958/9 enabled the hatch to be decked over and used as further vehicle space, increasing the capacity to 34 average sized cars. The passenger accommodation consisted of a large lounge fitted with row after row of bus type seating, more reminiscent of a cinema or hospital waiting room than a traditional steamer saloon, and fastidious passengers tended to choose the rather cluttered open deck in preference to joining the coughing throng in the cheerless smoke filled cavern below. A tea-room and a bar were also provided. British Polar two-stroke diesel engines powered the twin screws, and gave a top speed of around 15.5 knots.

The first of the three ships, the Denny-built *Arran*, inaugurated the Gourock-Dunoon service on 4 January 1954 and was followed by *Cowal*, from the Ailsa yard, Troon, on 9 April. Such was the demand on the Gourock-Dunoon run that *Arran* only appeared on the Ardrossan-Brodick service on peak Saturday forenoons or in the event of an emergency. *Cowal* opened the Wemyss Bay-Rothesay car ferry service on 1 October 1954 and was succeeded on the run by *Bute*, the last of the trio, in December. *Arran* was retained on the upper firth to cover relief sailings on these two routes. *Glen Sannox*, a larger and improved version of the ABC trio, built specifically for the Arran run, entered service on 29 June 1957 and completed the planned modernisation of the Gourock-Dunoon, Wemyss Bay-Rothesay, Wemyss Bay-Fairlie-Millport (Cumbrae), and Ardrossan/Fairlie-Brodick routes to car-ferry operation. Thus commenced the long era of state owned Clyde side-loading ferries, whose inherent restrictions bedevil the efficient operation of the first two above mentioned routes to this day.

Plate 79. Pioneer Clyde Car Ferry *Arran*. As these vessels also had to replace the cargo steamers, full cargo handling gear was also fitted abaft the car hoist. (Alan Brown collection)

Plate 80. *Arran* loading cars at Dunoon. The lift had its own ramps and thus the vessel could use any suitable pier. The system was very slow in operation, and could not handle the large commercial vehicles coming into use in the sixties. (G.E.Langmuir)

Plate 81. This view of *Arran* shows clearly the stern derricks and 'goalpost' designed for handling containers, barrows and cargo. By 1959 these had been removed, increasing car capacity from 26 to 35. (Ralston)

Clyde car-ferry developments

During the mid-sixties the CSP gave further thought to the improvement of their booming Clyde car-ferry traffic and proposals were advanced for the construction of two new vessels very similar to *Glen Sannox*, but with additional vehicle deck headroom. Although the side-loading system had increasingly shown its limitations the decision to retain it was principally based on the costs involved in converting the existing terminals to end loading, together with the flexibility of being able to use any pier in the event of emergency. The pier owners were financially unable — and perhaps a little unwilling — to spend any substantial sums of money on modernising their terminals and this financial lethargy supported the continuation of the status quo.

In one of the periodical upheavals of the state owned transport network a new Edinburgh based transport authority dominated by bus interests, the Scottish Transport Group, was formed to take over from 1 January 1969 the operation and development of the nationalised road and sea passenger transport networks in Scotland. The steamer services were thus isolated from their traditional railway associations and background and the Caledonian Steam Packet Co. Ltd., together with the railway piers at Craigendoran, Gourock, Wemyss Bay, Largs and Fairlie, were transferred to the Scottish Transport Group, along with the 50% railway holding in David MacBrayne Ltd. The remaining 50%, held by Coast Lines Ltd., was purchased by the STG in 1969, making MacBrayne's a wholly owned subsidiary of the STG. This had some interesting repercussions, since it amalgamated to all intents and purposes the CSP and MacBrayne operations under common overall control. Although nothing had come of the previous CSP proposals for two new side loading vessels the plans were resurrected and submitted to their new masters early in 1969, but being road orientated the STG realised that the slow, side-loading system, with its inevitable delays at peak periods and restrictions on the size and tonnage of commercial vehicles, had no real future and

was merely a short term expediency. In their eyes, the inadequacy of the Clyde vehicle ferries required urgent reappraisal, not merely a continuation of the present obsolete system, and once again the CSP proposals came to nought. The route subject to maximum delays at peak periods was to Arran — more and more visitors to the island were now finding it impossible even to contemplate a holiday without their car — and it was to this service the STG initially turned its attention. Provision was made for end loading linkspans to be erected at both terminals and *Glen Sannox* underwent some rather drastic rear-end surgery during her 1969 annual overhaul, when the stern bulwarks were cut away and a hydraulically operated stern ramp installed. However, the group were intent on providing a drive-through service and a second hand car/passenger ferry of this type was purchased. In their haste, coupled with inexperience in shipping matters, they could hardly have made a worse choice. A Swedish vessel, the *Stena Baltica,* happened to be available and in spite of being too small, too slow and having too deep a draught was purchased and brought to the Clyde, where Board of Trade bureaucrats gleefully pointed out that the ship did not comply with British standards. Extensive and expensive modifications were necessary before the vessel, now renamed *Caledonia,* inaugurate●! the new "drive through" service between Ardrossan and Brodick at the end of May 1970. *Caledonia* quickly revealed her faults and in spite of her improved facilities for vehicular traffic was the subject of much unfavourable comment by passengers. The next step was to review the Gourock-Dunoon and Wemyss Bay-Rothesay routes and the feasibility and costs of providing drive through facilities at these terminals was investigated by a firm of civil engineering consultants. However, the local authorities responsible for financing the projects at Dunoon and Rothesay were still reluctant to commit themselves to the very heavy capital expenditure involved and it is at this point a newcomer entered the scene to compete with the established operators.

Western Ferries

Western Ferries Ltd., was formed in 1967 by a group of Scottish businessmen, having special shipping and road haulage interests, to facilitate the carriage of road vehicles to and from the islands of Islay and Jura, off the western Scottish mainland. The principal industry of Islay is the distillation of whisky, which, together with farming, generates a considerable import/export traffic. Transport costs thus played an important part in the island economies and it was felt that a door-to-door service, using road vehicles ferried to and from the nearest feasible point on the mainland via a roll-on roll-off vessel, would effect a marked saving in time, handling, breakage, pilfering, dues and hence the overall transport costs. None of the MacBrayne vessels servicing the islands had special facilities for the transport of motor vehicles and since the company had shown little urgency in providing such accommodation Western Ferries decided the time was now ripe to step in. A small stern loading vehicle ferry with only limited passenger accommodation was accordingly ordered and on 7 April 1968 *Sound of Islay* inaugurated a roll-on roll-off service between Kennacraig, about half-way down the southern shore of West Loch Tarbert, and Port Askaig, Islay. Western Ferries' policy was to cut costs to a minimum and provide a basic reliable service, and with this end in view *Sound of Islay* was designed primarily as a commercial vehicle ferry in which convenience of vehicle loading was not subordinated to elaborate passenger and crew accommodation. Since the operation was essentially road vehicle orientated the shore terminals, devoid of all unnecessary frills, were located to give the shortest possible crossing consistent with overall convenience. The new service was an immediate success and captured a considerable amount of traffic, not only from the MacBrayne mail/cargo vessels, but also by conveying in trailers some of the bulk cargoes previously shipped by puffers. Lower rates ensured a general increase in trade and *Sound of Islay* quickly proved to be too small and too slow, particularly as the new facilities were being exploited to the utmost by James Mundell, a local haulier. With the benefit of experience it was obvious that a larger vessel with drive-through operation should have been built and Western Ferries didn't hesitate. A larger, faster and less utilitarian vessel was ordered from a Norwegian shipyard and *Sound of Jura,* as the new vessel was christened, took over from 1 August 1969. Meanwhile, a modified tank landing craft, the *Sound of Gigha,* inaugurated the Islay-Jura link across the narrow Sound of Islay between Port Askaig and Feolin, thus effectively linking Jura to the mainland via Islay.

When the success of the Western Ferries operation to Islay and Jura had been established, MacBrayne, supported by the Government, decided to introduce their own roll-on roll-off service and in November 1968 ordered a £740,000 passenger and vehicle ferry (*Sound of Jura* cost £315,000!) for the route. However, with the STG having both the CSP Co., and David MacBrayne unders its wing some juggling of ships was possible and following a £40,000 refit the *MV Arran* was transferred to the West Tarbert-Islay run on Monday 19 January 1970. The subsequent politically motivated battle between the efficient and initially profitable private enterprise Western ferries and state financed STG, at monumental expense to the taxpayer, has no place in this book, but it eventually resulted in Western Ferries withdrawing from the route in September 1981.

An Ancient Ferry Revived

Having successfully established themselves on the Islay run Western Ferries looked around for further opportunities to establish Norwegian type ferry operations on the west coast of Scotland, and in particular any which would give better car access to Tarbert, Loch Fyne and further boost the Islay traffic. Plans for a vehicular service across the Clyde from the Renfrewshire coast to Dunoon or thereabouts were first announced in September 1969, with McInroy's Point, between Gourock and Cloch Point, and Hunter's Quay, at the mouth of the Holy Loch, as the favoured terminal points. News of the STG's intention to replace their existing mail vessel on the Islay service with a roll-on roll-off ferry had of course reached the ears of Western Ferries and whether their announcement was intended as a preliminary warning to the state owned group to think again, otherwise retaliation in the CSP's own front garden could be expected, is perhaps conjectural, but in the event it proved to be no idle threat. The Cloch-Dunoon passage had been used from earliest times, particularly by drovers ferrying cattle and sheep to and from Cowal, since it afforded the most direct and convenient connection across the firth and was thus eminently suitable for a vehicular ferry service. McInroy's Point had the advantage over Cloch Point in being sheltered by the latter from the prevailing south westerly winds, although still somewhat exposed to the less frequent

northerlies, whilst Hunters Quay was similarly better protected than the more vulnerable pier at Dunoon. In spite of the STG going ahead and replacing the passenger/cargo *MV Lochiel* in January 1970 with the car ferry *Arran* on the West Tarbert-Islay run nothing further was heard at the time from Western Ferries on the subject of the proposed Clyde service.

The transfer of *Arran* left a gap in the Clyde car-ferry ranks and this was filled by the brand new *Iona,* originally intended for the Islay run and now reallocated to the Gourock-Dunoon route. The CSP officials could scarcely believe their good fortune in this new lamps for old exchange, even though common sense suggested it was scarcely likely to be more than a temporary expedient. *Iona,* with a bow door, stern ramp and side loading hoist was indeed a Jack of all Piers, and created quite a sensation when she made her maiden voyage to Dunoon on 29 May 1970, although the slow hoist and lack of a bow turntable resulted in bad timekeeping despite very liberal schedules. The unexpected acquisition of such a large and relatively luxurious vessel also provided a powerful lever to wean the Dunoon Town Council away from Western Ferries, since the latter initially wanted to use the small, utilitarian *Sound of Islay* on their proposed Clyde crossing. In spite of the procrastination by Dunoon Town Council over the provision of end-loading facilities the CSP decided to construct a stern loading ramp at the now little used south end of Gourock pier, the most sheltered position available with potentially reasonable road access and an acceptable proximity to the railway station. This step had been more or less forced on the company since an alternative mainland end-loading berth for the Arran boat was essential in the event of Ardrossan becoming inaccessible due to stress of weather. Work began in March 1971 and *Iona* commenced stern-loading at the new ramp from 26 July 1971, although of course she still having to side load via her hoist at Dunoon. In the autumn of 1971 Dunoon Town Council again rejected the installation of an end-loading ramp, mainly on the grounds of expense, but also because of the fear of damage occurring under adverse weather conditions. At the same time Western Ferries confirmed their previous intention to introduce a McInroy's Point-Cowal service and proposed to Dunoon Town Council a scheme to adapt Dunoon pier to take a Western Ferries end-loading vessel. The company had developed its own form of linkspan which was much simpler in design and cheaper in construction compared with other types, affording a saving of some 50% in capital expenditure, although the earlier models suffered from teething troubles and required expensive maintenance. The cost of the Dunoon structure was estimated to be not more than £50,000 and the provisions made by the company were that their annual costs should not, as a result, greatly exceed the gross annual cost of developing and servicing Hunters Quay and that the facilities should be available by 1 April 1972. Determined to eradicate this threat to their monopoly the CSP immediately produced its own counter proposals. They offered to provide a 45 minute interval two ship service if Dunoon would install a side loading linkspan on the pier and thus eliminate the hoist loading delays. To sweeten this expensive pill — the cost to Dunoon Town Council would be at least three times that of the Western Ferries scheme — the CSP would in turn transfer the large and luxurious *Glen Sannox,* which had already been fitted with a stern ramp, to the route and convert the passenger vessel *Maid of Cumbrae* to a stern/side loading (without hoist) car ferry.

That, at least, is the conventional explanation, but there may be a good deal more to it than that. Although Dunoon Town Council were obviously involved it appears that the CSP, as the ferry operator, was eligible for financial assistance towards the cost of terminals, and that plans and costings were obtained for both side and end loading ramps. In the case of end loading, the proposal was to build a causeway from the old coal pier (to the north of Dunoon pier), terminating in a south facing linkspan at the north end of the pier, somewhat in the manner of the rough sketch shown below. However, since this was a more expensive alternative, (reputedly at least £200,000 against the £150,000 estimate for side loading) financial assistance was only forthcoming for the cheaper version. This may have been a not unwelcome outcome, particularly so far as the CSP was concerned, since a side loading linkspan would be much more protected than the south facing one in adverse conditions.

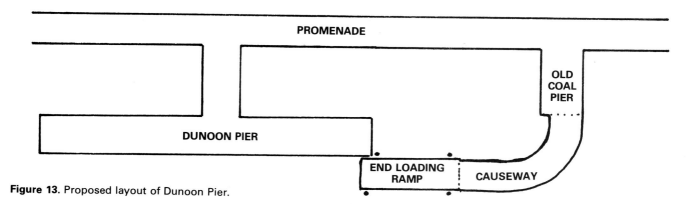

Figure 13. Proposed layout of Dunoon Pier.

Western Ferries must have danced with joy at this proposed retention of side loading, since it would obviously commit the Gourock-Dunoon route to this method for many years to come and even if their own scheme was rejected in favour of the CSP proposals the adherence to side loading would still make the development of a McInroy's Point-Hunters Quay drive-through service a viable proposition. The climax came on 6 December, when the Town Council invited representatives from both companies to put forward their respective schemes at a meeting specially convened for the purpose. On paper Western Ferries hadn't a chance, but the CSP had not entirely endeared itself to the local authorities in the past, and in fact it proved to be a very close run thing, with the casting vote of the Provost deciding the issue in favour of the CSP scheme. An adjustable side loading ramp was to be provided at the north end of Dunoon pier, at a cost of approximately £180,000, which the Town Council graciously offered the use of to Western Ferries. This kind offer was equally graciously refused, since Western Ferries considered it would be more sensible, economical and convenient to develop their own end loading facilities at Hunters Quay, and on 17 March 1972 they announced their intention of opening a McInroy's Point-Hunters Quay service in the autumn. Preliminary work on the terminals began in April. Once again Dunoon had failed to grasp the end-loading nettle, and the following extract from the CSP 1972 Annual Report makes interesting reading:

"Dunoon Burgh Council are to be commended for their vision in adopting this principle (a ramp at right angles to the face of the pier for use in conjunction with side ramps in the vessels)."

Some vision!

Although Government financial support for the state-owned Clyde and West Highland shipping services was readily forthcoming the Bute Ferry Company, owned by the Marquis of Bute, was quite unable to obtain a grant to improve its own ferry to the island and in December 1969 sold out to the STG. Having mopped up the Bute opposition, such as it was, the STG decided in 1972 the time had

now come to eliminate the Islay and (potential) Clyde opposition by putting in a take-over bid for Western Ferries. An offer of £2.00 per share was made in October of that year and later increased to £2.25. Although the Board recommended acceptance there was a strong feeling that Western Ferries should remain as an independent competitor and the anti take-over lobby, led by Sir William Lithgow, received a great deal of support. In addition, since a so-called Conservative government was then in power it was felt that private enterprise might at least get a fairer deal. The STG bid was conditional on acceptance by 76% of the shareholders, with a deadline of 30 October, and when this failed the Dornoch Shipping Company (a member of the Lithgow Group) made an alternative offer of the same amount, which was accepted. Some major shareholders sold out but others, including a number with distillery interests, came in and the company was reconstructed as Western Ferries (Argyll) Ltd. Following this reorganisation Western Ferries announced that the McInroy's Point-Hunters Quay service would be introduced in the spring of 1973. Two short distance Swedish end-loading drive-through ferries, the *Olandssund III and IV* were purchased and after being stormbound at Stavanger for a spell eventually reached the Clyde in March and April 1973. *Sound of Shuna* (ex-*Olandssund IV*) ran trials on 16 April 1973 and tested the linkspans at Hunters Quay and McInroy's Point on 4 and 15 May respectively. She then opened the new service on 3 June 1973, giving an hourly service each way until 14 July, when she was joined by *Sound of Scarba* (ex-*Oslandssund III*) and a half-hourly service introduced. Meanwhile, the 45 minute interval Gourock-Dunoon service, operated by *Glen Sannox* and *Maid of Cumbrae*, had opened on 27 May 1972, *Iona* having been posted to the West Highlands and *Bute* and *Cowal* transferred to work an improved Wemyss Bay-Rothesay timetable. Some four years later Rothesay Harbour Trust accepted (once again by the casting vote of the Provost) CSP proposals for up-dating the side loading facilities by the introduction of a variable height ramp similar to that at Dunoon and which eventually came into operation in the summer of 1977.

Plate 82. *La Maddalina,* built for Genoese owners, was the prototype from which the hull form and Voith Schneider propulsion layout for the Clyde ferries *Juno* and *Jupiter* were based.
(E.C.Goldsworthy & Co.)

Voith Schneider on the Clyde

During the 'sixties Captain Goldsworthy had given considerable thought to the question of ensuring the continuity of his business as Voith Schneider agent for Great Britain and what was left of the Commonwealth. There was inevitably a time approaching when he would no longer be capable of coping with the physically demanding field work involved during the construction, trials and commissioning periods of British built Voith Schneider propelled ships and it was thus imperative to find a suitable assistant or assistants. As a result, Mr Norman Almy, a naval architect and engineer trained at Thorneycroft's Southampton, came to the company in December 1964 and was joined in January 1968 by Mr Jonathan Mason, a master mariner. Both Mr Almy and Mr Mason were offered a share of the business on a partnership basis as from 1 January 1969 and therefore became equally involved with Captain Goldsworthy in spreading the gospel — and, more importantly, in gaining converts!

As mentioned previously, the small Voith Schneider passenger ferry *Rose* had been transferred from the Thames to the Clyde in the spring of 1967 and had subsequently given excellent service on the Largs-Cumbrae service. Captain Goldsworthy and Mr Mason visited Gourock shortly after the acquisition of *Rose* (renamed *Keppel* by the CSP) and were able to give the engineers some advice concerning the operation and maintenance of this type of propeller. During their visit Captain Sinclair, the CSP, Marine Superintendent, mentioned the Kyle of Lochalsh-Kyleakin (Skye) service (a Gourock responsibility since January 1945 and transferred to CSP ownership in 1957) and enquired whether Voith Schneider propulsion would be suitable for the new vessels being planned for that service. Fortunately, Captain Goldsworthy had visited and studied the operation of the route some two years previously, and was able to reassure Captain Sinclair that with double ended Voith Schneider propelled ferries he could quadruple the present traffic with the same number of vessels, a statement subsequently proved correct when two VSP ferries came into service 18 months later.

Following the success of the Skye ferries the CSP marine superintendent realised the potential of Voith Schneider propulsion for the Clyde services, particularly in cutting down manoeuvring and berthing times. Shortly afterwards, in September 1971, proposals for a new vessel suitable for the Gourock-Dunoon run were put forward and a general arrangement drawing for a twin screw vessel with controllable pitch propellers and bow thrust unit was prepared as a basis for investigation. However, the issue had been complicated by the insistence on the vessel having a Class 2 passenger certificate. A Class 2, for Gourock-Dunoon? No, not for Gourock-Dunoon, but to permit her use on the Outer Isles (Stornaway) run! In spite of this proviso E.C. Goldsworthy & Co., were asked to submit proposals for a VSP vessel capable of operating a half-hourly service on the four-mile Gourock-Dunoon crossing and were able to show that a 14 knot double-ended ferry could maintain a half-hourly cycle even with a full load of cars and passengers. In the ensuing discussions the CSP officials admitted that whilst the proposal was very attractive they were not prepared to countenance double-ended operation on the Gourock-Dunoon run. Their opposition was based on the grounds that while the vessel was berthed at Dunoon the south facing ramp could be exposed to waves of up to 8ft high and that in their view a pointed bow was essential. As a result of these deliberations an asymmetrical vessel with centrally mounted bow and stern units was recommended, based on the Genoese owned *La Maddelina*, but having a conventional bow instead of a bow ramp. Because of new DTI regulations requiring a passenger deck above a car deck to be heavily insulated in case of fire, plus the headroom required for high vehicles, an open car deck was also preferred. By 13 October a specification had been drawn up for a single ended vessel having either two controllable pitch propellers plus a bow thruster, or two Voith Schneider propellers, in both cases with diesel-electric drive. Voith immediately pointed out that diesel-electric drive was an unnecessary expense and that direct diesel drive would be just as effective. Voith Schneider propulsion was now deemed essential for a single ended vessel if the 30 minute service requirements were to be met, but to show that they had investigated all possibilities the CSP officials had to have alternative proposals and costings to put before the STG committee. A number of timings were made on the run with *Iona,* a 16 knot vessel, which indicated that a 30 minute service was not a practical proposition with a screw propelled vessel. The Gourock marine staff were also able to persuade the Edinburgh bus seat sailors that to insist on a Class 2 certificate for a vessel intended mainly for the Gourock-Dunoon run was an expensive folly, and Class 4 and 5 certification was agreed. Although the Outer Islands requirement was relaxed for this vessel, it was by no means forgotten.

In view of the commitment to side-loading at Dunoon, referred to earlier, an asymmetrical vessel, having a normal bow, stern and side ramps, and powered by two Voith Schneider units bow and stern on the centre line of the vessel, was ordered from James Lamont & Co. Ltd., Port Glasgow. A lines plan was provided by Voith and in view of the heavy penalty clause on speed, tank tests were carried out at Teddington. The design work was prepared for the shipyard by Keel Marine. Inevitably, the launching of the new vessel was seriously delayed by strikes and it was not until 27 November 1973 that *Jupiter* finally entered the water. Trials were run off Skelmorlie on 12 March, when a mean speed of 14.52 knots was attained over four runs — well in excess of the 14 knot contract. Further tests resulted in 13.5 knots being recorded when going astern, and 3 knots sideways! The centrally mounted propellers afforded a number of advantages over offset ones, including improved course stability, a slightly better speed, and an unimpeded thrust from the propellers in all directions. Passenger accommodation was located forward, with a long open car deck aft, and each Voith Schneider unit received its energy from a 1220 hp Mirrlees Blackstone four-stroke diesel engine. Although *Jupiter* bears little external resemblance to *La Maddalina,* being larger and with quite different passenger and vehicle accommodation, the machinery layout and hull lines of the Italian ship formed the model from which the Clyde vessel evolved.

Jupiter entered service on 19 March, when the ease and rapidity with which she was able to manoeuvre and berth at both terminals was demonstrated to the full. In spite of being single ended, having to back onto the Gourock linkspan and side load at Dunoon, she was able to maintain the half hour schedule without difficulty provided no large vehicles were carried. However, the problems side-loading/unloading large coaches and articulated lorries, particularly at times of heavy traffic, soon became obvious and resulted in delays. Initially, the side ramps were located right at the forward end of the car deck, leaving articulated lorries with no deck space in which to swing when embarking or disembarking, but this design error was spotted and corrected prior to the vessel entering service.

Plate 84. *Jupiter* side loading at Dunoon. This compromise in layout is still less efficient as proper drive through operation. (Alan Brown collection)

Plate 85. (Bottom). *Saturn* at Dunoon. The third of the trio was of a rather different appearance and somewhat less successful than her elder sisters. However, the extension of the upper deck beyond the bridge was a pleasing and appreciated improvement. (Alan Brown collection)

Juno

An early intimation that a second ferry similar in design to *Jupiter* was in the pipeline came in April 1972; indeed, plans had been submitted to the DTI for approval by that date, and some equipment already ordered. The STG were very anxious to replace the existing mail boat on the Stornaway run with a roll-on roll-off vessel, possibly on a shorter route, and it was for this service that the new ferry was intended. The very fact that a design of this type was put forward for Class 2 passenger certificate approval seems rather strange, and perhaps indicated some political manoeuvring between the CSP and 'Edinburgh'. Not surprisingly, the DTI refused to accept the 'Jupiter' design for Class 2 certification on the grounds of:

1. Unsuitable design
2. Vessel insufficiently strong
3. The forward Voith Schneider propeller insufficiently immersed for such an exposed route

The DTI response effectively scotched any hope of using this second vessel on the Stornaway run and the STG's first reaction was to cancel the order and build in its place a stronger vessel with twin screw propulsion. However, as cancellation costs were involved, the CSP marine superintendent was instructed to report to the STG board on Monday 7 August with details of these so that a decision could be made whether to proceed or cancel. Now came some delicate political skirmishing; the board wished to cancel but were deterred by the costs involved whilst the CSP wanted the second ferry for the Wemyss Bay-Rothesay route but couldn't use that argument since it didn't form part of the planned £1,280,000 expansion and renewal programme. In the event, the board was unable to settle this issue and in spite of further meetings on 11, 15, 17 and 29 August no conclusion could be reached. However, on the latter date light at the end of the tunnel became faintly visible and it was agreed to see whether, by juggling around with the various vessels up and down the west coast, something could be found to take over the Stornaway run. An announcement was expected by 6 or 7 September, but in the event a decision was not reached until the end of the month.

This decreed that *Clansman*, the MacBrayne winter relief ship, was to be lengthened by adding a 30ft section amidships, the superstructure raised by about 5ft 6ins, the deck strengthened and a bow visor and stern door added to permit drive-through operation. *Iona*, transferred from the Clyde, opened the new Ullapool-Stornaway route in March 1973 and *Clansman* took over

from her in June of that year. Having cleared that hurdle, the Gourock men now pressed hard for the second Clyde ferry and after a further month's vacillation their wish was granted — the order was to proceed. The vessel, christened *Juno,* was launched on 16 September 1974 and as no progress had been made regarding linkspans at Wemyss Bay or Rothesay it was announced she was to be used on the Gourock-Dunoon run. *Juno* attained a mean of 14.375 knots on trial and entered service on 2 December 1974.

The Wemyss Bay and Rothesay terminals were eventually converted to linkspan operation in May and June 1977 respectively, with side loading at Rothesay, and a third ferry, *Saturn,* similar but not identical to the Gourock-Dunoon pair, took over from *Glen Sannox* in February 1978. Slight changes in bow form, propellers and engine room layout all apparently combined to adversely affect her speed as she attained a mean of only 13.88 knots on trial. These were held on 27 January 1978, off Skelmorlie, the actual timings and speeds being:

Run	Direction	Time	Speed	Mean of Pair	Mean of Four
1	S	4m 25s	13.59k	13.905k	
2	N	4m 13s	14.22k		13.88
3	S	4m 20s	13.84k	13.87k	
4	N	4m 19s	13.90k		

In spite of these disappointing results the vessel was accepted, but it would be fair to say she has proved to be the least successful of the trio.

With the acquisition of *Saturn* the pattern of the Caledonian MacBrayne upper firth car ferry services on traditional routes was established for the next one and a half decades. Although not direct descendents of *Lymington* — cousins perhaps — I have dealt with the background of these three vehicles in some detail since they inaugurated the Voith Schneider car ferry concept on the Firth of Clyde and also introduced into Great Britain the asymmetrical hull form with bow and stern propellers mounted on the centre line of the vessel. It now seems incredible that the two Gourock-Dunoon 'streakers', as *Jupiter* and *Juno* are affectionately known, were originally conceived for, of all places, an Outer Isles service.

With the CSP and MacBrayne companies now wholly owned subsidiaries of the STG there seemed little point in retaining both as separate entities, other than for tax purposes, and in 1973 the two were amalgamated under the present trading title of Caledonian MacBrayne Ltd.

CHAPTER 8

SOUND OF SANDA

Lymington was taken over by Western Ferries (Argyll) Ltd., together with all relevant papers, spares and stores as agreed between the company and British Rail, at noon on 25 March 1974. A Western Ferries crew, under the command of Captain David Neill, now well known as the skipper of the preserved paddle steamer *Waverley*, had travelled down to Portsmouth to collect their new acquisition and bring her back to the Clyde. They departed from the Camber at 15.15 for ramp and handling trials and following satisfactory completion of these proceeded to Husband's shipyard, Marchwood, where the vessel was to be prepared for her journey north. Work commenced next day, including the fitting of radar and a Decca Navigator and by mid-day on the 29th she was ready for inspection by the salvage surveyor and DTI officials. Following completion of compass adjustments at 15.30 she headed down Southampton Water and turned west for the long trip back to the land of her birth. A log of the voyage is given in Appendix 1.

Plate 86. *Lymington* at Kilmun after her voyage from the south.　　　　(J.Hendy collection)

Plate 87. In the Garvel dry dock at Greenock *Lymington* is being refitted and converted for her new role. The ramps used on the Solent slipways have been cut away and will be replaced by short ones to suit the link spans at Hunters Quay and McInroys Point.　　　(D.Robertson)

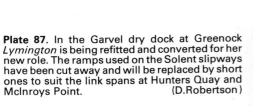

Plate 88. *Sound of Sanda* at Hunters Quay.
(Alan Brown collection)

Into Service

Lymington arrived safely at Hunters Quay on 2 April and lay at Kilmun pier for almost three weeks before moving to the James Watt dock, Greenock on 23 April in readiness for a major overhaul. She entered the Garvel dry-dock on the following day and for the next four months was in the hands of Scott's, the Greenock shipbuilders and repairers. The wooden passenger decks above the sponson houses were replaced by steel and the whole ship shot blasted, primed and painted in the Western Ferries colours of red hull, white upperworks and dark blue funnels sporting the company's logo. Since *Lymington* would be working from Western Ferries own design of linkspan the original heavy, folding ramps were removed and replaced by small hydraulically operated ones. These new ramps are slightly offset and equipped with hooks which engage with a locking bar on the linkspan itself, whilst steel hawsers gave additional safety and prevent the vessel from swinging. It was suggested that one of the original ramps be retained to permit landing on beaches or slipways but this was not accepted since it would have prevented drive-through operation on the ferry service. The two lifeboats were removed and replaced by a new small fibreglass boat and 4 inflatable life-rafts in order to retain the Class 4 certificate. At the time of *Lymington's* purchase the company were also actively investigating the introduction of a commercial vehicle only drive-through ferry between McInroy's Point and Bute (Port Bannatyne), for which a Class 4 certificate was necessary. In the event, apparently due to objections by Port Bannatyne residents, the project was abandoned, but the Class 4 did enable her to operate to Rothesay, Ardyne, Loch Striven, etc., as required. *Lymington,* now renamed *Sound of Sanda,* emerged from dry dock on 1 August and on the 22nd carried out trials, including berthing at both terminals. Her manoeuvrability and ease of handling delighted all concerned, and following some rough weather runs on the 23rd she took over the ferry service from 19.15, in more moderate conditions. Some minor teething troubles were experienced with the ramps on the following day, which necessitated a return to the shipyard for investigations and remedial work. She duly returned to service on the evening of 30 August and spent the whole of the next day on the run with complete satisfaction. A training voyage up river took place on 3 September, leaving Kilmun at 9.30 and arriving Stobcross Quay, Glasgow 13.05, and after a 2¾ hour break she returned to Kilmun and tied up for the night at 19.20. Further familiarisation runs with Western Ferry masters were carried out on the 4th and 5th, and from the 12th she became regularly employed on the ferry, normally berthing overnight at Kilmun pier.

Plate 89. Hunters Quay. *Sound of Sanda* loading at low water. She operates with a crew of only four.
(Alan Brown collection)

Plate 90. (Bottom left). Leaving Rothesay for Inchmarnock as described in the text on the next page.
(A. McRobb)

Plate 91. (Bottom right). Through the Kyles. Note the Colintraive/Rhubodach ferry in the background. (A. McRobb)

Propeller modernisation

The new propellers fitted in 1955 still incorporated blade shaft needle roller bearings and leather seals, but later models were fitted with plain bearings and Buna (synthetic) se ' British Rail had considered modernising *Lymington's* propellers during the 1967/68 winter overhaul, but since it was intended at the time to replace her in 1970/71 no action was taken. In the event, she was given a five year extension after undergoing an extensive overhaul and in view of this the necessary parts were ordered from Voith to enable the three propellers to be converted. However, when sold to Western Ferries only one had been modified and had then been in service for two years without the need for any seal changes. At Western Ferries' request the spare propeller was overhauled and modified by BR at Southampton and subsequently fitted to *Sound of Sanda* when in the Greenock dry-dock. In addition, BR supplied all the spares and instructions for modifying the third propeller.

Although *Sound of Sanda* was intended as a relief vessel the continuing increase in traffic often meant that all three ships had to be pressed into service at peak periods and by 1983 she was working virtually the same hours as the other two. Charter work was also increasing and included Rothesay-Ardyne, McInroy's Point-Holy Loch (USA base), and McInroy's Point-Loch Striven. Because of her wooden car deck the 'Sanda' was ideally suited for the transport of road tankers carrying liquid nitrogen to the USA base and to Loch Striven.

Through the Kyles

One of *Sound of Sanda's* most interesting excursions took place on Tuesday 23 September 1975 when she was chartered to collect cattle and sheep from Inchmarnock, an island lying off the west coast of Bute. She left Kilmun at 6.20am, sailing through the Kyles of Bute and then anchoring off the island until the tide made. As there was no slipway on the island the *'Sanda'* had to be carefully manoeuvred as close as possible inshore and long stout wooden planks run from the bow ramp onto the beach. Loading the 55 cattle and 48 sheep took just under 1½ hours and a further hour was spent at anchor until all the drovers had embarked. The livestock disembarked at Rothesay via a small slipway at the end of Berth 1A and *Sound of Sanda* eventually tied up at Kilmun at 20.32. Captain Neill summed it up in the following words: "It was one hell of a day!" She also had a spell of about one month, from 11 January to 14 February, transporting stores and materials from Rothesay to Ardyne, berthing overnight at one or the other, with an occasional return to Hunters Quay when work was on the slack side.

Plate 92. Happier days for *Waverley* with *Sound of Sanda* alongside. Captain David Neill, who has commanded both vessels, can just be seen under the bridge. Yards of film would be exposed to capture for posterity this unique double berthing. (T. Cooper collection)

Plate 93. (Bottom). Two important parts of our maritime heritage. *Sound of Sanda* hoves to, allowing *Waverley* to speed past. (Alan Brown collection)

An eventful night

The normal tranquility of Clyde pleasure steamer sailings was rudely shattered on the afternoon of Friday 15 July 1977. The paddle steamer *Waverley*, returning to Dunoon from a cruise to Loch Goil had the misfortune to strike the Gantock rocks, off Dunoon, on a falling spring tide and became stranded. Passengers were safely evacuated by the ships' lifeboats and Western Ferries' *Sound of Shuna*, which managed to manoeuvre alongside the starboard paddle box. Thanks to heavy duty pumps brought alongside by the American navy *Waverley* was kept afloat, and fears that she might break her back proved to be unfounded. *Sound of Sanda* was brought out from Kilmun in the evening and after first crossing to McInroy's Point to pick up a *Waverley* director, tied up at Dunoon to stand-by and assist as necessary. Just to add to the general gloom it poured with rain all night, but at about midnight *Waverley* slipped off the rocks and under her own steam was beached next to the Dunoon coal jetty. Once the excitement had died down and *Waverley* was safe 'Sanda's' part in the proceedings was almost over, and at about 02.00 she crossed back to McInroy's Point and then returned to her berth at Kilmun.

Sound of Sanda renewed her acquaintance with *Waverley* on Saturday 15 September 1979 when the latter called at Kilmun on a PSPS charter. *Waverley* was due at the Holy Loch around 12.20 and 'Sanda' lay off to allow the paddler to come alongside the pier. *Sound of Sanda* then berthed alongside *Waverley* for half an hour before moving off again to let her guest depart at 13.20.

A more nostalgic reunion took place in May 1981 when one of her old Solent consorts visited her at Kilmun. Following the Gantocks grounding, enquiries were made as to whether it would be possible to charter the Portsmouth-Ryde passenger vessel *Shanklin* for a short period to cover *Waverley's* programme of Clyde sailings. This proved to be impossible in view of her own south coast commitments and in the event the much smaller and slower *Queen of Scots* ran a modified programme of excursions under charter to Waverley Excursions Ltd. The temporary loss of *Waverley* at the height of the season had highlighted the vulnerability of a single ship operation and when *Shanklin* became available in the autumn of 1980, following a lengthly withdrawal due to engine failure, she was snapped up by the Waverley team. Although mainly intended for service on the Bristol Channel, *Shanklin*, now renamed *Prince Ivanhoe*, was programmed for two weeks Clyde cruising in late May/early June 1981, and on Sunday 24 May cruised from Glasgow to Dunoon via the Holy Loch. Waiting at Kilmun pier to welcome her old companion was *Sound of Sanda*, a strange rendezvous indeed for the two Denny built ex-Isle of Wight ferries, both having spent the major portion of their lives within the confines of the Solent under the same railway ownership.

U-Turn on the Clyde

The year 1981 also marked a further example of Govermental inconsistency and muddle which ended in fiasco. CalMac were in receipt of a large Government subsidy (£5.8 million in 1981), part of which related to the Gourock-Dunoon service, and Western Ferries felt that they too were entitled to a few crumbs from this very substantial cake. Following representations by Western Ferries, a statement was made in Parliament on 2 July intimating that the Secretary of State for Scotland proposed to withdraw the CalMac Gourock-Dunoon service subsidy and offer Western Ferries a capital grant of £300,000 to purchase an extra car ferry for their Hunters Quay-McInroy's Point service. In addition Western Ferries agreed to provide a passenger only service between Gourock and Dunoon with their 'fast ferry' *Highland Seabird,* which would qualify for a subsidy during its first year of operation. Thereafter, if Western Ferries decided to discontinue the *Highland Seabird* service foot passengers would be conveyed by a through Dunoon-Gourock bus service via the Hunters Quay-McInroy's Point crossing.

The Secretary of State's announcement caused a furore at Dunoon, where various vested interests and pro-CalMac lobbies combined to oppose these plans, and CalMac themselves neatly exploited the reaction by announcing their intention to withdraw from the route after Saturday 17 October. The weak link in the Western Ferries scheme undoubtedly lay in the use of *Highland Seabird,* since the Dunoon commutors rightly considered it to be completely unsuitable on account of its limited capacity and potential berthing problems in anything other than a flat calm. If the use of *Highland Seabird* had been intended as a sop to the commutors pending introduction of the through bus service it backfired badly, and by 18 August some 376 objections to the proposals had been received by the secretary of the Scottish Transport Users Consultative Committee. Their report, published on 17 September, concluded there would be "serious hardship, inconvenience and difficulty" to travellers if CalMac were to withdraw their service and they also doubted whether Western Ferries would be able to operate a reliable service with *Highland Seabird.* Whilst they were undoubtedly correct about *Highland Seabird,* it is difficult to see what "serious hardship, inconvenience and difficulty" would be caused by a through bus service. Indeed, with picking up points at Kirn and Hunters Quay, it

may well have been quicker and *more* convenient. However, as an old tutor of mine used to say, "You've only got to make sure you get the right persons on a committee to obtain the result you require!"

In view of this opposition Mr Younger, the Secretary of State, soon showed his skill in the art of fudge making. On Sunday 11 October he announced that Western Ferries were to operate the vehicle service and CalMac would carry passengers only, whilst on the 23rd Mr Rifkind, defending his superior's decision, said CalMac would have to find a suitable passenger only ferry and, if need be, sell *Jupiter* and *Juno.* By 5 November this had become watered down to the Government now being willing to consider subsidising a CalMac Gourock-Dunoon passenger service as long as the company competed "in the market place" with Western Ferries for vehicle traffic.

CalMac, of course, were quick to see which way the wind was blowing and continued to operate as normal after 17 October. The Secretary of State's U-turn was completed on 13 February 1982 when a passenger only subsidy of £250,000 to CalMac for their Gourock-Dunoon route was announced — in other words, CalMac would just carry on as before, except that they were now only allowed to advertise an hourly service. Naturally, CalMac had found it quite impossible to obtain a passenger only ship for the run and in our 'Alice in Wonderland' world of subsidies, grants, write-offs, etc., the subsidised passengers and unsubsidised vehicles are carried on the same ship at the same time.

What happened to the additional ship for Western Ferries? This was none other than *Lymington's* old paddle consort, *Farringford,* transferred from the Sunny Solent to the bleak north-east coast in 1974, and now redundant following the completion of that monumental Folly, the Humber Bridge, in June 1981. On the strength of Mr Younger's undertaking to pay £300,000 towards its costs Western Ferries duly completed purchase of *Farringford* in October 1981 and proposed converting her from paddle to either Voith Schneider or Schottel propulsion. The vessel remained laid-up at Hull during the winter and, following the Secretary of State's U-turn Western Ferries were left with an unwanted vessel on their hands. She was finally sold by Havelet International Ltd., to John Hewitt, Heddon, Hull, who took delivery on 5 March 1984, and the vessel was broken up at Silcock's Basin, Hull shortly afterwards.

Plate 95. (Bottom). *Farringford* finished her days on the Humber, and is seen here at New Holland. The ramps were removed for the Humber service as were the rudders at the 'bow'. She was actually purchased for Western Ferries after ceasing Humber service in 1981, but fate (and the Secretary of State for Scotland) decreed that she was not to join her old Lymington consort on the Clyde. (G. Reed)

Plate 94. *Prince Ivanhoe* renews acquaintance with an old Solent fleet-mate as she approaches Kilmun. (Alan Brown collection)

Plate 96. Cruise leaflet.

Cruise Ship

Sound of Sanda's first taste of cruising came on Sunday 29 July 1984 when she was given the honour of operating a special Western Ferries staff cruise to view the Tall Ships Parade off the Tail o' the Bank. In the following year local hoteliers complained about the lack of evening cruise facilities, formerly a very popular Clyde summer season feature. In response Western Ferries decided to operate cruises out of Hunters Quay on Wednesday evenings during the height of the season, this generally being a free evening when no other organised entertainment was provided. *Sound of Sanda* was chosen as the cruise vessel for a number of reasons, namely:

1. She had the smallest vehicle capacity of the three ships and was therefore the one which could be most easily spared from the ferry run.
2. She had the best and most easily adaptable passenger accommodation.
3. Facilities for the dispensation of tea, coffee and light refreshments were available, together with a bar.
4. She was the most interesting ship and the one with the most character.

'Sanda' was dressed with bunting from the top of the main masts to each corner, and wooden boards were erected at the for'd end of the deck houses to form a windbreak, with an access gap at one side. Of course, no one can possibly be expected to enjoy a cruise nowadays without being subjected to "musical entertainment", and Western Ferries proved to be fully competent in this aspect. Music for dancing was provided by a man with an accordian, or a three piece band, whilst the canned variety ensured there was no respite in the lounges. At least one woman was found in tears, unable to escape the perpetual ear shattering blast! Cruises were of 3 hour duration, leaving Hunters Quay at 19.30 and returning at 22.30. The distance steamed varied between 21 and 23 miles, at an average speed of 7.75 knots and details are tabulated below:

Cruise	Date	Destination	Pass	Weather
1	Wed 26 June	Loch Goil	80	O'cast. Rain am
2	Wed 3 July	Gareloch. Faslane	49	O'Cast
3	Wed 10 July	Loch Goil	—	O'cast
4	Wed 17 July	Loch Goil	27	O'cast. Heavy rain
5	Wed 24 July	Loch Goil	24	O'cast. Drizzle
6	Wed 31 July	Rothesay Bay	91	Cloudy. Fine
7	Wed 7 Aug	Loch Goil	—	O'cast. Drizzle
8	Mon. 12 Aug	Loch Goil	85	Cloudy
9	Wed 14 Aug	Loch Goil	32	O'cast. Heavy rain
10	Wed 28 Aug	Gareloch	83	Cloudy. Fine
11	Wed 4 Sept	Loch Goil	76	O'cast. Drizzle

Note: All cruises non-landing. Loch Goil cruises to off Carrick Castle.

Plate 97. *Sponson* saloon on *Sound of Sanda.* (Alan Brown collection)

The cruise to Carrick Castle is probably the most attractive marine excursion on the upper firth, and one which can only be appreciated from the deck of a steamer. The narrow entry into Loch Goil, and the setting of the castle itself, are particularly dramatic, and it was unfortunate that the summer of 1985 was one of the wettest on record. As could only be expected, this dismal weather had a marked effect on passenger numbers but nevertheless the experiment was considered successful and was again repeated in 1986. In addition to the public excursions a cruise for the company's staff was also given on Wednesday 4 September to Loch Long, Loch Goil, and Holy Loch.

During her annual overhaul in November 1984 at Clyde Ship Repairers, Renfrew, *Sound of Sanda's* wheelhouse was broken into and the telegraph, compass and binnacle and deck leveller all stolen. Replacements were fitted but, as Captain MacArthur remarked, "the wheelhouse had lost its character". Some three months later an alert member of the constabulary spotted a ship's telegraph, compass and binnacle while patrolling "The Barrows" — the famous Glasgow market. The law took its course and the items were duly restored to their rightful place in 'Sanda's' wheelhouse. On another occasion the brass builders plate, which formerly faced the car deck under the bridge, was removed when the vessel lay at Kilmun but unfortunately it has not so far been recovered.

Plate 98. Builders' and commemorative plaques. (Alan Brown collection)

Plate 99. *Sound of Sanda* becomes *Sound of Santa* for Christmas (Capt. K. McArthur)

Sound of Seil

By the mid-80's Western Ferries service and charter traffic had continued to expand to the point where *Sound of Sanda* was becoming too small to cope with the demand. In particular, lorries and coaches were increasing in size and weight, and one juggernaut left space for only five cars, since the deck was insufficiently wide to permit a row of cars to be parked alongside. This limitation was especially embarrassing during the morning and evening peak commuter periods and Western Ferries decided the time had come to acquire an additional larger vessel. The 'Sanda' could then be demoted to a true 'spare' vessel, but kept in readiness for use at short notice. *Fishbourne* and *Camber Queen,* with their limited passenger accommodation and maximum car capacity would have been ideal, but at the time they were available Western Ferries were still recovering from the 1981 fiasco and the opportunity was missed. However, the 'Sanda's' old Lymington consort, *Freshwater.* had also been withdrawn in late 1983, when *Caedmon* was transferred from the Fishbourne route, and sold to H.G. Pound the following year. After lying at Tipner Wharf, Portsmouth, for about 12 months she was again sold under circumstances somewhat reminiscent of the 'Emperor of China's' Clyde steamer purchases at the time of the American Civil War. A mysterious Lebanese gentleman, who found it necessary to travel and to remain incognito due to the political situation in war-torn Beirut, eventually reached England's once green and pleasant land and purchased *Freshwater*. According to Pound's, the vessel was to be used as a ferry on the 50 mile crossing between Cyprus and Turkey — a statement greeted with some hilarity by Island commutors who had suffered from her 50 minute Ryde-Portsmouth crossing in the winter of 1982! (see Chapter 9). However, rumour had it that her actual destination was to be Beirut

itself, for use as a beach landing craft by the Lebanese Christian Militia, which provoked further ribald comment from the local Isle of Wight Commutors Militia. . In response to enquiries a spokesman from the Lebanese Embassy said they had no contact with the Christian Militia and declined to make any further comment. Rumour or fact — who knows? Whatever her intended role it is perhaps significant that she never left Portsmouth and was purchased from her Lebanese owner (now identified as one Anis Abiad, reputed to be a dealer in heavy machinery and construction equipment), in December 1985 by Western Ferries for a rather less exciting career on the Firth of Clyde. She was towed to Husband's shipyard, Marchwood, and taken over on 5 February 1986 by a Western Ferries crew under the command of Captain James Addison. Following preparation at Husband's for the voyage north she left Southampton on Tuesday 1 April and immediately ran into heavy weather. After sheltering in Poole Bay overnight she refuelled at Plymouth on the Wednesday evening and following an adverse weather forecast at 18.00 hours next day altered course for Milford Haven. Here she remained stormbound until Sunday 13th, when she finally got away at 07.00, and after a 5-minute stop at McInroy's Point late on Monday evening berthed at Renfrew Harbour at 01.25 on 15 April.

The following two months were spent undergoing modifications, including replacement of the heavy folding ramps by the smaller, hydraulically operated Western Ferries pattern, and cutting away the overhanging sun deck to permit two lorries or coaches to park side by side on the car deck. Now renamed *Sound of Seil*, she left Renfrew on Monday 16 June and following linkspan tests and training runs made her inaugural service run on the 14.30 ex-Hunters Quay on Wednesday 18 June. *Sound of Seil's* extra capacity has had a remarkable effect on the traffic using the Hunters Quay-McInroy's Point route, and has proved to be a most valuable acquisition.

Plate 100. *Freshwater* at Renfrew undergoing conversion. The side doors cut into the bulwarks to allow her to relieve *Farringford* for overhaul on the Humber can clearly be seen.

Plate 101. (Below) The Crossley 8-cylinder two stroke engines fitted to *Freshwater/Sound of Seil*. (Capt. A.Eadie)

Plate 102. (Below right). *Sound of Seil* in service. She is the largest Western Ferries vessel and it is fitting that her Lymington and Hunters Quay precursor should still be sailing as her consort. (Capt. A.Eadie)

Management Buy-out

In April 1985 the Clyde services of Western Ferries (Argyll) Ltd., were separated from the parent company and the Lithgow Group and other shareholders bought out by a group operating under the BES scheme. The new company, Western Ferries (Clyde) Ltd., is a wholly owned subsidiary of Harrisons (Clyde) Ltd., who had been the managers of the previous company for some years. The only service now operated by Western Ferries (Argyll) Ltd., is the Islay-Jura route.

Cruises

Western Ferries repeated their evening cruises during the 1986 season to the same timings and destinations as in 1985. *Sound of Sanda* operated only one of these plus a private 'Crossroads' charter to Loch Goil and the Holy Loch on Saturday 31 May. Under the command of Captain Jim Wilson she left Hunters Quay at 18.15 and sailed past Carrick Castle, and turned off Lochgoilhead, before retracing her route down Loch Goil and Loch Long and into the Holy Loch. She also made the first of the public cruises, on Wednesday 18 June, to Carrick Castle and the Holy Loch, under Captain Ken MacArthur. Although rather cloudy the evening was fine and clear and she covered the 22½ miles at an average speed of 7.76 knots. The remainder of the public cruises were operated by *Sound of Seil*, but once again the weather was generally adverse and they were not subsequently repeated.

During the 1986 and '87 seasons *Sound of Sanda* was rather less in evidence and spent a good deal of her time moored off Kilmun, although still earning her keep on reliefs, extra sailings and charter work. The construction of a new 'temporary' pier at Port Menai, Loch Long, in connection with the Trident base at Coulport brought work for her in transporting steelwork, etc., during the building period. Perhaps the most interesting of the 1987 charters, however, was the Scott Lithgow contract for *Sound of Seil* to ferry workmen each morning and evening between Inchgreen Dock, Greenock and the oil rig *Ocean Alliance* anchored off the Tail o' the Bank. To provide extra seating *Sound of Seil* embarked one or two coaches each evening at McInroy's Point before proceeding up-river and then unloaded these after completion of the following morning's charter — a similar arrangement to her spell on the Portsmouth-Ryde service in 1982! The initial 10 week charter commenced in early November but at the time of writing (late February 1988) it is still in operation.

During this period *Sound of Sanda* has been regularly in service on the ferry, covering the morning and evening absences of *Sound of Seil*, in addition to operating a number of Holy Loch charters.

Overhaul 1988

A considerable amount of work was done during *Sound of Sanda's* 1988 overhaul which commenced on Tuesday 5 January at Clyde Ship Repairers Renfrew Yard. The original asbestos insulation was removed from the engine room bulkheads in the lower saloons and replaced by a less lethal substitute. The Ruston 3 cylinder diesel engine driving the remaining original generator set was replaced by a Perkins unit, the change-over being effected by cutting out a side section of the hull and welding in a new plate after the transplant. The car deck above the engine room had previously been plated over and the wooden decking relaid in 1970, and this year the remaining sections were dealt with in a similar manner. 'Elephant's feet' for shackling down heavy lorries were also incorporated in the new decking.

'Sanda's future

The extensive overhaul carried out augers well for *Sound of Sanda's* future, which now depends rather more on charters than on passage work and it is to be hoped that sufficient work in connection with the construction of the Trident base at Coulport, plus her usual charters, will keep her economically occupied. Although her speed is now down to between 7 and 8 knots the main engines and Voith Schneider units appear to be in reasonable condition and whilst spares for both are still available they are on long delivery and at a price.

It is perhaps a pity that no special celebrations are envisaged to honour her 50th birthday but one can well appreciate the reluctance of the owners to commit their stand-by vessel on a busy holiday week-end in case she should be required for duty at short notice. The two main anniversary dates fall on the Easter and May holiday week-ends and the *MV Columba's* Largs-Oban and Oban-Iona cruises over Easter, plus *PS Waverley's* May holiday week-end sailings in the West Highlands are powerful counter attractions to any local cruise by *Sound of Sanda*. However, it is to be hoped she will be given an airing on the ferry run on Sunday 1 May, the same day and date as that on which she made her maiden voyage 50 years ago between Lymington and Yarmouth.

Plate 103. (Left). *Sound of Sanda's* W.H.Allen engines still give yeoman service fifty years after entering service. Many more modern vessels have had to be re-engined.   (Alan Brown collection)

Plate 104. (Below). *Sound of Sanda* cruising with suitable decor of flags and bunting.   (Capt. A.Eadie)

THE LYMINGTON LEGACY

In spite of her early problems *Lymington* had convincingly demonstrated the outstanding and unique handling characteristics of Voith Schneider propulsion, and her influence on the design of later ferries, on the Solent and elsewhere, cannot be over-emphasised. Indeed, a measure of this can be gauged from the fact that whereas in 1958 the railway owned Solent car ferry fleet comprised one Voith Schneider, one paddle and three double twin screw vessels, in 1988 all seven Sealink vessels (including the withdrawn *Cuthred*) are Voith. On the Firth of Clyde there was not a single Voith Schneider propelled vessel in 1958; thirty years later the score is one twin screw, two double single screw, and ten Voith! The development of the Solent and Firth of Clyde car ferry fleets up to the introduction of Voith Schneider vessels has been considered previously and this final chapter is devoted to the further changes which have taken place up to the present time.

The reasons for the adoption of diesel-electric paddle propulsion in the case of *Farringford,* the second double-ended ferry built for the Lymington-Yarmouth service, have already been explained; suffice to say here that this design was not repeated. Once the reliability of *Lymington's* vertically mounted replacement propellers had been established there was no hesitation in specifying Voith Schneider propulsion for the third vessel, and *Freshwater* was in effect an enlarged version of *Lymington.* Although after her introduction *Lymington* was demoted to 'spare' vessel, this was simply due to her smaller capacity; in any case 'spare' was a bit of a misnomer, for during the busy summer season and winter overhaul periods she was fully employed on relief duties.

The first major development of the post-war era took place on the Portsmouth-Fishbourne route. The private car 'explosion' plus the ever increasing amount of goods delivered to the island by road vehicles in the 'fifties was overwhelming the three ferries, then approaching their 30th birthdays, and bookings for the passage were having to be made months in advance. Consequently British Railways, in conjunction with Portsmouth City Council and the Isle of Wight County Council, decided in 1957 to completely reorganise the service at a total overall cost of £1 million, no mean investment in those days. The capacity of the route was to be enlarged by:
1) Increasing the number of crossings.
2) Reducing the time on passage.
3) Reducing the turn-round times.
4) Increasing the capacity of the ferries.

Since the existing slipways were unsuitable for use by larger vessels a completely new terminal with offices, car parking and a large slipway was built at Portsmouth 'round the corner' in the Outer Camber docks. These new facilities eliminated the nuisance and conjestion caused by waiting vehicles in Broad Street, and ferries now berthed clear of the entrance to the Camber. In addition a new slipway was constructed at Fishbourne, facing seawards instead of across the creek, together with a large parking area on the old approach road. Two new Voith Schneider ferries were built by Philips of Dartmouth, very similar in design to *Freshwater* but with a reduced passenger capacity (165 against 620) and correspondingly increased car capacity (34 against 28). The same type of Crossley EGN8/65 two stroke diesel engines were fitted, giving a speed of

10½ knots. This increase in speed over the older vessels, together with the much improved manoeuvrability, decreased the passage time from 60 to just over 35 minutes. *Fishbourne,* the first of the two vessels, inaugurated the new service on 7 July, although some training runs and berthing trials had been carried out previously. In fact, the new slipways were completed and put into use prior to the delivery of *Fishbourne,* and even with the older, slower ferries a marked increase in traffic resulted. *Camber Queen,* the second ferry, entered service on Tuesday 28 August, her maiden voyage marking the completion of the modernisation programme. The peak period service was increased to provide hourly departures in each direction and for the first time the service was advertised to carry foot passengers. (Previously pedestrians had been carried, but were not encouraged).

Fishbourne and *Camber Queen* were rarely seen other than on the Portsmouth-Fishbourne route, but very occasionally they called at Yarmouth in the event of Fishbourne being inaccessible. For example, shortly after entering service, *Fishbourne* grounded at Fishbourne on 5 September 1961 and *Camber Queen* sailed to Yarmouth until the slipway was cleared. During the very severe winter of 1963 ice in Wootton Creek resulted in the service having to be transferred to Yarmouth for a few days at the end of January. This was not due to the vessels being unable to reach Fishbourne, but simply because the ice packed up alongside the hull, blocking the engine cooling water inlets and causing engine overheating. Again, on the week-end of 14/15 February 1975 the Portsmouth-Fishbourne service was suspended for essential repairs at Fishbourne slip-way and a special service operated between Portsmouth and Yarmouth from 16.00 hours on the Saturday. The passage time was about 2 hours in each direction.

Traffic continued to expand during the 'sixties and the number of cars carried to the island during the months of June, July and August alone increased from 54,919 in 1963 to 59,982 in 1964. Although *Lymington* was being used as a 'spare' vessel for both services this increase in traffic was beginning to warrant an extra vessel on the route. In addition, the Portsmouth-Ryde passenger service was being operated by two coal fired 13 knot paddle steamers, *(Sandown* and *Ryde),* and three 14 knot motor vessels, *(Southsea, Brading and Shanklin),* and the management was anxious to dispose of at least one of the paddlers. Passenger traffic on the route was exceptionally heavy at peak summer week-ends but much lighter for the remainder of the year, and with the steady decline in cruise traffic the two paddlers were really only required on about half a dozen peak Saturdays.

During the 1964/65 winter a particularly interesting project, related to the berthing and gangway tests carried out by *Freshwater* and *Farringford* at Portsmouth Harbour and Ryde Piers in 1964, was seriously considered. What the management had in mind was a new passenger/vehicle ferry capable of maintaining the Portsmouth-Ryde passenger schedule in step with the other vessels and operating the Portsmouth-Fishbourne service at other times. The suggested dimensions were 185ft length x 35ft beam, x 6ft 6ins draft, and a speed of 14 knots. Voith Schneider propulsion was considered essential, but with the propellers driven by constant speed

Plate 105. The old regime struggles on as work commences on the new Fishbourne slipway, built to face seawards. (R.Butcher)

Plate 106. The new slipway at Fishbourne with *Fishbourne (II)* testing prior to entering service, on 6th July 1961. (R.Butcher)

Plate 107. (above). *Camber Queen* at Broad Street, Portsmouth. Note the staggered saloon layout to allow maximum car carrying capacity. (R. Silsbury)

Plate 108. An icebound scene in the winter of 1963/64. This problem resulted in Yarmouth being used as the Island destination for a short time. (R. Butcher)

alternating current electric motors supplied by three diesel-alternator sets. An alternative scheme using four rotatable propeller units was put forward by Schottel, each unit (two forward and two aft) being driven by its own diesel engine and although considerably cheaper in first cost than the diesel-electric proposal it is believed the use of four separate engine rooms was not favourably regarded by B.R. Investigations continued throughout the winter but in June 1965 a spokesman revealed that whilst they had hoped to have the new vessel in service in 1966 a vehicle-carrying hovercraft service was now also being investigated. This proposition effectively put paid to the dual purpose vessel for the time being and

one of the paddlers *(Sandown)* was withdrawn at the end of the 1965 season without replacement, the loss of capacity being partly made up by a more intensive working of the three motor ships. In the event the hovercraft idea was abandoned, since British Rail had come to the conclusion there was no economic future for this mode of transport in carrying large numbers of cars and passengers on the short runs to the Isle of Wight. In their opinion, the economics of this form of travel were at that time only favourable to hovercraft where distances of over 100 miles were involved — a decision which must have been greeted with relief by residents and holidaymakers alike on the grounds of noise alone.

Plate 109. Oops! *Cuthred* stuck on the slipway at Broad Street. Note the London registration of the 'C' class now that Sealink activies are controlled from Liverpool Street. The Schneider unit is just visible.
(Alan Brown collection)

The 'C' ship era

The three original vessels, *Fishbourne (1)*, *Wootton* and *Hilsea* had been sold early in 1962 to H.G. Pounds, the Portsmouth shipbreakers, (all were subsequently resold) and although *Lymington* was now officially 'spare' vessel for both the Fishbourne and Yarmouth services, the continuing increase in traffic on both routes now definitely warranted a further vessel for the Fishbourne run. This time there was no talk of building a dual purpose vessel capable of maintaining station on the Portsmouth-Ryde route since the principal requirement was now additional lorry and commercial vehicle space. The order was announced in June 1968 and the new vessel, built by Richards of Lowestoft and named *Cuthred*, arrived at Portsmouth twelve months later. *Cuthred* marked a major change in design, since she was not only larger, having a capacity for 400 passengers and 48 cars, but the accommodation layout was quite different. A large lounge, accommodating 131 passengers and complete with snack counter and bar, extended across the whole width of the ship above the car deck whilst lower deck lounges, described by the "Shipbuilding & Shipping Record" reporter as "claustrophobic", provided seating for a further 178. Open decks, well equipped with seating, extended fore and aft of the upper lounge. Propulsion was by two Voith Schneider propellers, each driven by a 300hp Paxman 8RPHCM diesel engine, a remarkably low output for such a large vessel, and *Cuthred* was soon found to be decidedly underpowered.

The inexorable rise in traffic on both routes again made the provision of extra capacity essential and in 1971 BR decided to order three further vessels similar to *Cuthred* but with increased engine power. One of these was earmarked as an additional vessel for the Fishbourne route but the other two were intended to replace *Lymington* and *Farringford* at Lymington, as mentioned in Chapter 6. The trio, ordered from Robb Caledon Shipbuilders Ltd., Dundee, were launched on 3 May, 1 June and 29 June 1973 and received the names *Caedmon*, *Cenwulf* and *Cenred* respectively. The first, *Caedmon*, entered service at Portsmouth in July, just in time for the summer peak, but it was not until September and November that *Cenwulf* and *Cenred* arrived at Lymington. With an individual capacity for 750 passengers and 52 cars the new Lymington pair tripled and doubled the respective total passenger and vehicle capacity of the two older ships. Propulsion was by two Voith Schneider 16/100 units, each driven by a 400hp Mirrlees Blackstone

ERS6M diesel engine (a substantial increase in power over *Cuthred's* 300hp Paxmans), giving a speed of about 11 knots.

In 1974, *Cenwulf* and *Cenred's* first full year in service, passenger figures for the Yarmouth route topped the one million mark for the first time, setting the stage for a major reconstruction of the terminals. Work at Lymington commenced in 1976, when marshland to the east of the pier was reclaimed to provide additional parking, together with new entrance and exit roads. A linkspan and adjacent pier complete with covered pedestrian walkway and powered gangways extended downstream from beyond the station and replaced the original concrete slipway. Figures for the year again showed an increase to 1,176,030 passengers, 192,804 cars and 19,752 commercial vehicles. Progress at Yarmouth was slower and it was not until January 1980 that Yarmouth Harbour Commissioners announced the long awaited improvement scheme. Financial problems caused further delays and it was only after the Government agreed in November 1981 to release money for the £1.5 million scheme that the project finally got under way. An existing slipway was enlarged for temporary use by the ferries, and a new linkspan constructed, together with modifications to the quay on the site of the existing slipway. The new facilities were eventually opened in September 1983.

Returning to 1976, the 50th anniversary of car ferry operation between Portsmouth and Fishbourne was celebrated on 21 April. A cavalcade of vintage vehicles, led by a 1929 Leyland open top double deck bus and followed by a further 14 old cars, lorries and motor cycles, embarked on the gaily beflagged *Caedmon* at Portsmouth for the crossing to Fishbourne. Following a brief circuit of the island terminal the party then returned to the mainland on the same vessel.

During 1977/78 hydraulically operated mezzanine decks were installed on all four 'C' class ships, enlarging the vehicle capacity from 52 to 70 cars. On the Yarmouth route traffic figures for 1979 showed a further increase to 1,323,525 passengers, 225,412 cars and 28,523 commercial vehicles, the surge in the latter being attributed to many island farmers now using Salisbury as their main cattle mart. Incidentally, from 1 January 1969 until 31 December 1978 the railway marine activities had been designated the Shipping & International Services Division of British Rail but from 1 January 1979 the title *Sealink* was adopted and henceforth came into common use.

Plate 110 (Top). *Freshwater* approaches Yarmouth after slipway widening. (R.Stewart)

Plate 111. (Centre). *Cenwulf* in Lymington the river. She could carry 52 cars, double that of the *Lymington*, but after mezzazine decks were added in 1977/78 the capacity went up to 70! (R.Stewart)

Plate 112. (Left) *Caedmon* loading at Fishbourne. The hydraulic rams for lifting the ramps can clearly be seen. (R.Stewart)

Plate 113. The new link span at Lymington from the air with one of the 'C' class berthed.   (R.Stewart)

Plate 114. Approaching the new Lymington link span. *Freshwater* lies off the old slipway to the left.   (R.Stewart)

Plate 115. The 150th Anniversary Celebrations of the Lymington-Yarmouth route with Whitbread horses disembarking from *Cenred* at Yarmouth.
(R.Stewart)

Plate 117. (opposite page). Broad Street, showing the congested Camber with *Caedmon* approaching the slip after the departure of either *Fishbourne* or *Camber Queen*.   (R.Stewart)

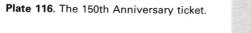

Plate 116. The 150th Anniversary ticket.

LYMINGTON-YARMOUTH
1830-1980

**COMMEMORATIVE CELEBRATION
SATURDAY, 7TH JUNE**

Since the withdrawal of *Farringford* the route has been 100% Voith Schneider, and when one recalls the problems experienced by *Lymington* in her early days it is rather ironic that since 1965 Sealink has no longer found it necessary to dredge the Lymington river. Not because the river no longer silts up, but simply because they can rely on the scouring action of the Voith Schneider propellers to keep the channel clear!

Saturday 7 June 1980 marked the 150th anniversary of the first, regular, steam powered ferry between Lymington and Yarmouth and this historic event was celebrated in style. A cavalcade of vintage vehicles and bicycles left Brockenhurst station in the morning for Lymington where *Cenred*, dressed overall, waited to convey them to Yarmouth. Here, an official reception greeted the vessel, and a further collection of old cars joined their mainland contemporaries for a tour of west Wight. Historic motors were much in evidence that day, and Sealink's special guests were transported by a vintage bus to the Farringford Hotel, Freshwater, where lunch awaited them. Meanwhile, a Ferry Boat Fayre with displays, stalls and sideshows was getting under way at the harbour, where the 103 year old steam engine *Freshwater*, once owned by the old Freshwater, Yarmouth and Newport Railway and formerly a familiar sight at Yarmouth was exhibited by the Isle of Wight Steam Railway. It was rather a pity that *Lymington*, a most important landmark in the history of the service, was not present.

With the arrival in 1983 of the new vessels for the Fishbourne service *Caedmon* was transferred to Lymington and *Freshwater* withdrawn. For the past five years the three sisters (or should it be brothers?) have maintained the west Wight service and whilst rumours of replacement vessels circulate at present no plans have yet been officially announced.

Broad Street Blues

In spite of the four vessel shuttle service and all-night operation during summer peak week-ends the total volume of traffic using Broad Street had long outstripped the capacity of the terminal to handle it comfortably. Broad Street itself was often choked with queues of vehicles overflowing the terminal's limited parking space, much to the annoyance of the local residents, and the ferries themselves were often fully booked months ahead during the busy holiday season. In addition, with *Cuthred* and *Caedmon*, the maximum had been reached in the size of vessels capable of using the berth. If one of the ferries became stranded on a slipway — which they did — then the result was utter chaos.

Salvation came in the unlikely guise of a power station closure. A former dry dock on the opposite side of the Camber, subsequently converted to import coal for the Gunwharf Road power station prior to oil-fuel conversion, was purchased by Portsmouth City Council when the station closed down. Negotiations between British Rail and the City Council resulted in agreement being reached for a new ferry terminal to be built on the site of this old dock complex. To cover the cost the council had to raise a £2 million loan and BR agreed to reimburse the city its £374,000 annual payment over the next 20 years, with BR also being responsible for all maintenance costs. The agreement opened the way to a complete revolution of the Portsmouth-Fishbourne service, permitting the use of larger vessels and linkspan loading and involved:-

1) The construction of a new terminal complex in Gunwharf Road, complete with offices, waiting room, ticket office, refreshment room, stores, car park and linkspan.
2) The building of one, and probably two, new ferries to the maximum possible size, followed by a further one or two vessels as found necessary.
3) The conversion of the Fishbourne terminal to linkspan operation.

Linkspans of the neutral buoyancy tank type were chosen for the terminals, allowing the ferries themselves to employ short ramps in place of the heavy, folding pattern necessary for slipway use and as the linkspans were unaffected by wave movement it was planned to install one at the end of **Ryde** pier in addition to that at Fishbourne. The intention was to operate one large ship between Portsmouth and Ryde during peak periods and in the high summer season carrying booked and pre-paid cars only. Three trips every two hours were scheduled, and to avoid any danger of congestion in the town no ticket office was to be provided at Ryde, since all traffic other than that previously booked and paid for would travel via Fishbourne. Contrary to expectations nothing further was heard of this intriguing scheme.

Work commenced at Portsmouth in June 1979, when buildings were cleared from the former dock site, and four years later the Lord Mayor officially opened the new complex following completion of the terminal buildings. The linkspan had in fact been in operation for more than a year, the first car to use it being driven on and off *Fishbourne (II)* by Ray Butcher, the present Terminal Supervisor, during prow trials in January 1982. Whilst the new mainland terminal was seen to be a desirable improvement over the previous facilities it was a quite different story on the island; the Ryde car ferry plan had been quietly dropped, and Sealink's Fishbourne proposals met with a hostile reception from local residents. Their main worries were that major dredging of the channel for the new jumbo ferries could lead to structural damage of Creekside homes and additional noise, disturbance and nuisance caused by the increased volume of traffic. Sealink first attempted to allay their fears with honeyed words and when this approach failed brought out the big stick. The IW Services manager in November 1979 warned the natives that failure to modernise the Fishbourne terminal and introduce new ferries on the route could lead to island residents concessionary fares being withdrawn and a County Press headline "Warning of Dearer Fares if Sealink's Plans Fail" spread fear and consternation throughout Wight. However, the Fishbourne and Wootton warriors remained singularly unimpressed by the threatened dire consequences if they failed to lay down their arms, and in April 1980 another petulant Sealink outburst blamed a "handful" of people for jeopardising their £10 million modernisation programme. In fact, all the opponents could really do was to delay the necessary Parliamentary approval and eventually they gave up the unequal struggle. The Bill went through on 27 July 1981 and Sealink's plans for two new ferries and terminal improvements were announced in the local press on Tuesday 8 September 1981, together with an artist's impression of the new vessels. Construction of the Fishbourne linkspan started in late August 1982 and was completed in June 1983. Dredging started in March, and was largely confined to widening and deepening the main channel, where some 78,000 cubic metres of material was removed. The first of the new ferries, *St Catherine*, entered service on Sunday 3 July — the beginning of phase 3 in the terminals history.

Plate 118. First car to be unloaded at the new Gun Wharf terminal linkspan, Portsmouth. Ray Butcher drives his own car off *Fishbourne* during pre-service tests. (R. Butcher)

Plate 121. (opposite page). *St Cecilia* in the new Sealink colours adopted after privatisation. The public relations boys had a field day explaining the profound significance of the new livery to the public. In spite of their efforts it quickly became known as the 'cigarette packet livery'. (John Hendy)

Plate 119. (Right). *Marechal de Toiras* — prototype for the 'Saints'. (E.C.Goldsworthy & Co.)

The Saints come sailing in.

During the period of changeover from slipway to linkspan operation *Fishbourne (II)*, *Camber Queen*, *Cuthred* and *Caedmon* continued to work from Broad Street until Saturday 20 February 1982 when the terminal closed after the final sailing of the day. The new terminal opened on the following morning, with temporary Portacabin accommodation, pending completion of the permanent facilities. Subsequent to the sale of *Shanklin* in November 1980, *Cuthred* had been used as a temporary replacement on the Portsmouth-Ryde service in the event of a passenger ferry breakdown, but passengers

complained that the saloon was too high up and the vessel rolled excessively. In response to these complaints Sealink transferred *Freshwater* to the route during the overhaul periods of *Southsea* and *Brading* in February and March 1982 and once again incurred the wrath of the island commutors. With crossing times extending to 45-50 minutes train connections were sometimes missed, and to speed up disembarkation an extra stairway was fitted between the car and boat decks. In addition, due to the limited undercover accommodation many passengers were forced to endure the rigours of bleak winter crossings on the open car deck and their vociferous

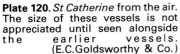

Plate 120. *St Catherine* from the air. The size of these vessels is not appreciated until seen alongside the earlier vessels. (E.C.Goldsworthy & Co.)

complaints resulted in a novel solution to the problem. On Sunday 28 February *Freshwater* made a special voyage to Fishbourne where two withdrawn Southern Vectis Bristol LH single deck buses were embarked to provide additional 'saloon' accommodation. They were eventually unloaded on Sunday 28 March, after having made more than 360 Solent crossings. History repeated itself when *Sound of Seil, ex-Freshwater,* again carried buses to provide additional passenger accommodation during her Greenock-*Ocean Alliance* oil rig charter during the 1987/8 winter.

Design work on the new ferries commenced in the late 'seventies and initially an enlarged and improved version of the 'C' class ferries was envisaged, having a length of 250ft, 7ft 6ins draft, and speed of 12-13 knots. The 2 hour round trip cycle was to be maintained by improved loading facilities at the terminals and reduced passage time, thus counterbalancing the greater vehicle and passenger capacity. However, difficulties were encountered in obtaining the necessary power within the draft limitations and Voith tentatively suggested an asymmetrical three propeller layout, with one bow and twin stern units. Feasibility studies were carried out for the following designs.

1) 2 VSP double ended
2) 3 VSP asymmetrical with bow and stern loading.
3) Twin CPP with a VSP bow thrust unit.

The board were interested in alternative 3) on the grounds of cost, but the whole of Sealink's Solent car ferry services literally revolved round the Voith Schneider propeller and the manager was convinced there was no satisfactory alternative to this method of propulsion. His reaction to the CPP proposal was one of horror: "If HQ provide me with such vessels I'll send them straight back to where they came from!" There was no need to worry — the feasibility study was merely done to convince the Board that the CPP proposal, although the cheapest, was simply not a practical proposition.

A three propeller vessel, the *Marechal de Toiras* was already operating between La Pallice and Ile de Re, in France, and following further discussions with Voith and a visit to La Pallice, Sealink's thoughts definitely hardened in favour of the three propeller proposal. The reason for the proposed 'turning circle' off Fishbourne now becomes clear!

Ministerial blessing for the two vessels was given in 1979 and shortly after the granting of Parliamentary approval for the Fishbourne scheme an order for the pair was placed with Henry Robb & Co., Ltd., Leith. The first, *St Catherine,* was launched on 30 March 1983 and delivered at Portsmouth on Friday 24 June. After inspection by Sealink officials she had to visit Husband's shipyard for some minor engine repairs and eventually entered service on Sunday 3 July. She caused a sensation. *Fishbourne (II)* and *Camber Queen* looked like toys in comparison, and one felt overawed by the sheer size of the vessel. A casual glance gave the impression of a double ender, since there were bow and stern ramps and a central funnel, but closer inspection revealed the asymmetrical nature of the design. The superstructure, with bridge mounted at the forward end, was set slightly towards the stern, and the bow, carrying the ships' name, distinguished by a pronounced flare. The design marked a fundamental departure from the 'Lymington' concept, the asymmetrical layout being the price which had to be paid to obtain the required capacity and speed within the draft limitations. The second, *St Helen,* took to the water on 14 September 1983 and arrived at Portsmouth 24 November. After trials on the Solent she entered service on Monday 28 November, and the official inauguration ceremony took place on 8 December, when a cavalcade of vintage vehicles boarded the vessel at Fishbourne. The opening ceremony of the new Fishbourne terminal was performed by Captain Wheeler, the IW Services manager at the same time.

The long awaited 'privatisation' of Sealink came to pass in the summer of 1984 when for a total sum of £66 million the Bermuda based Sea Containers group took over. Their new livery and insignia was revealed at the end of March, together with an infantile explanation of what it represented and the profound significance of it all. To the majority it merely signified a further step in the degeneration of good taste! The arrival of *St Catherine* heralded the withdrawal of *Fishbourne (II)* and similarly *Camber Queen* was withdrawn following the entry of *St Helen.* Both were sold for further service abroad, and although *Fishbourne* was eventually lost due to stress of weather, *Camber Queen* still survives under Portuguese ownership.

Some consideration had been given in 1979 to re-engining the sluggish *Cuthred,* whose lack of power meant she had to be withdrawn under adverse weather conditions. This was a serious embarrassment to Sealink, and the costs of modernisation were weighed against the estimated loss of revenue in order to determine the feasibility of the proposal. However, as the design of the new ships was then more or less completed it was probably felt expenditure of an obsolescent type of vessel could not really be justified and no action was taken. In their programme Sealink had forecast that a third vessel would be necessary in the late 'eighties, and possibly a fourth in the early 'nineties, and in early 1986 a third 'Saint' was ordered to replace *Cuthred.* An order for a new Sealink car ferry usually meant the kiss of death for the shipyard concerned! Philips, Robb Caledon and Henry Robb had all built their last ships, and it was understood that the order was going to Richards of Lowestoft, but final terms could not be agreed and at the last minute they withdrew. Choice was now becoming rather restricted and the Moving Finger moved on to Cochrane's Shipbuilders, of Selby. However, at the time of writing, they are still alive and well so perhaps privatisation had broken the dreaded 'Sealink Spell'.

The new ship was launched sideways into the River Ouse on 4 November 1986 and received the name *St Cecilia.* She arrived at Portsmouth on 18 March 1987 and made a trial crossing to Fishbourne at mid-day on the 21st, followed by an inaugural cruise on the 23rd. The Isle of Wight Symphony Orchestra provided music for the occasion, which must have been a welcome change from the usual pop group 'entertainment'. The arrival of *St Cecilia* marked the end of the road for *Cuthred* and she was withdrawn following the expiration of her Passenger Certificate on 30/1/87. In spite of a number of enquiries from prospective purchasers she still remains laid up at Lymington (March 1988).

All three vessels have proved to be comfortable, popular, good sea boats and reliable. The asymmetrical layout does not appear to have caused any problems, the vessels normally berthing stern first at Portsmouth and bow on at Fishbourne. A rapid 90° turn is made off the mouth of the Camber prior to backing up to the linkspan, and with torrents of foaming white water churning out sideways from bow and stern they present a spectacular example of Voith power and manoeuvrability at its most impressive. The effect of the three new ships on traffic has been remarkable, as the following rounded-off figures on the next page indicate.

Even during the 1987/88 winter, with two vessels in service, vehicles have been left behind due to lack of space and already there is talk of a fourth vessel being required soon. To paraphrase Parkinson's Law — car traffic will increase to fill the ferry space available! Demand has already outstripped capacity at Fishbourne, resulting in serious traffic problems in Fishbourne Lane (as forecast by the residents in 1980) and additional land has now been purchased to enlarge the terminal. Work is expected to commence in April 1988. It should be remembered that the figures quoted apply to Portsmouth-Fishbourne only, and that more and more vehicles continue to stream across to Cowes and Yarmouth also. Where will it all end?

Year	Vessels	Crossings	Passengers	Cars	Coaches	Goods Vehicles
1982	Fishbourne Camber Queen Cuthred Caedmon	10000	530000	165000	2200	27000
1984	St Catherine St Helen Cuthred	8000	710000	215000	4000	31000
1987	St Catherine St Helen St Cecilia	7000	920000	265000	5000	45000

Red Funnel Review

The evolution of Red Funnel car ferry services up to the outbreak of war in 1939 has been briefly covered in Chapter 1 and having now examined the post-war developments at Portsmouth and Lymington it is of interest to review progress at Southampton. The car ferry *Her Majesty* had been sunk during an air raid on Southampton in December 1940 and although subsequently raised was then scrapped. A post-war replacement was found in the form of a surplus tank landing craft, purchased in 1947 and suitably modified by the addition of passenger accommodation and side-loading doors at Thorneycroft's. Christened *Norris Castle*, the second Red Funnel vessel to bear the name, she proved to be a successful and important acquisition, providing the fundamental design on which the new generation passenger/vehicle ferries of the late 'fifties and 'sixties were based. Although at first used only during the summer months she commenced all year round operation in 1952 when she took over the cargo service from the veteran *Lord Elgin*. Initially vehicles were side loaded from the Southampton and West Cowes pontoons but circa 1950 a new buffer pontoon at Southampton and concrete slipway at East Cowes permitted use of the bow ramp. Side loading has been retained at West Cowes and is still used for the few cars and light vans using this terminal.

The influence of *Norris Castle* was seen when *Carisbrooke Castle* appeared in 1959, signalling the end of one era and the beginning of another. The first of the post-war ships, the 1949 *Balmoral*, had followed the pattern set by *Vecta* in 1939, being simply a passenger ship with accommodation for cars. *Carisbrooke Castle*, on the other hand, was a car ferry with accommodation for passengers, although this was more spacious and sumptuous than that of the Lymington-Yarmouth vessels. A similar, but improved version, the *Osborne Castle*, followed in 1962, allowing *Norris Castle* to be withdrawn and sold, and a third ship, virtually a repeat of *Osborne Castle* and named *Cowes Castle*, entered service in December 1965. However, the growing amount of commercial traffic resulted in some detail changes being made to the final member of the quartet, whose larger open foredeck and reduced passenger accommodation betrayed her LCT lineage. Appropriately, she re-introduced the ancestral name of *Norris Castle*, and as expected, was used mainly for the carriage of heavy goods vehicles on the direct Southampton-East Cowes service.

By the early 'seventies the ever increasing volume of traffic convinced the company that the future lay with drive-through vessels, and their next acquisition marked the end of the LCT based design. Exactly 45 years after *Fishbourne* entered service at Portsmouth, Red Funnel followed suit with their first double-ender. After a difficult and traumatic gestation *Netley Castle* finally entered service in late June 1972 and with centrally situated passenger accommodation over the car deck and bow and stern ramps she followed to a certain extent the style of the Portsmouth 'C' vessels. However, she presented a neater and less cumbersome appearance and differed by having a bridge at each end of the superstructure in place of the centrally mounted wheelhouse on the 'C's'. Until 1983, when the honour went to *St Catherine*, she was the largest of the Solent car ferries, and also had the distinction of introducing a novel form of propulsion for Isle of Wight vessels. Conventional twin screw propulsion, driven by a pair of Crossley 8-cylinder two-strokes, had powered the four previous 'Castle's' and for their double-ender Red Funnel had the choice of double twin screw, Voith Schneider or rotatable propeller propulsion. However, their experience with *Vecta* had soured their attitude to Voith Schneider and they plumped

for rotatable propellers. Four Aquamaster units, each driven by a 500hp V8 Caterpillar Tractor 4-stroke diesel engine, were positioned towards each 'corner' of the vessel, and provided propulsion and steering. Being double ended, the decision was rather surprising, since *Netley Castle* had far less need for the extra manoeuvrability afforded by these units than her single ended consorts, which had to back away from the slipways and then swing bow-first to their destinations. Indeed, since it had been publically announced that the ship would never need to turn round, one end was designated the Southampton end and the other the Cowes end instead of bow and stern. Port and starboard became east and west sides respectively. That may well have been the case but Ron Adams, in his excellent publication "Red Funnel — And Before" records a confusing occasion when he found himself travelling to Southampton with the Cowes' end leading!

Once *Netley Castle* had settled down into service after the inevitable teething troubles *Carisbrooke Castle* was withdrawn and sold. The tremendous convenience of drive through operation soon persuaded the management that something would have to be done about the three remaining vessels and in September 1975 their decision was announced. *Cowes Castle* and *Norris Castle* were both to be 'jumbo-ised' and converted to drive through operation over the 1975/76 winter. They were scarcely recognisable on their return, having been lengthened by 30ft., the car deck clearance height increased by 14ft and extra car space provided by stowable mezzanine decks.

The bow ramp was retained for use at East Cowes and gates installed across the cut away stern to allow drive through operation via a new linkspan at Southampton, located on the site of the existing slipway. Plans for a linkspan at Cowes fell through when the harbour authorities refused to allow this on the grounds that the vessel's stern, when berthed, would protrude into the fairway. The procedure was thus to stern load via the linkspan at Southampton, and load over the bow ramp and slipway at Cowes. This entailed swinging off Southampton and backing onto the linkspan, and backing off the slipway at East Cowes, and to assist in manoeuvring bow thrusters were fitted to both ships.

The Mark II *Cowes Castle* re-entered service in late December 1975, followed by *Norris Castle* in April 1976, and unlike most conversions were an undoubted improvement for both motorists and foot passengers. The new open deck above the Master's cabin, offering an unrestricted view ahead, was particularly appreciated on a fine day. *Netley Castle* had her 'Southampton end' ramp removed in 1976 and a stern gate fitted for linkspan use, and in 1980 additional car space was provided in the former west side casing. This also involved widening the hull into a sponson-like structure, giving the vessel a most unbalanced appearance when viewed end on.

With three drive-through ships now in operation *Osborne Castle* was withdrawn in the spring of 1976, but kept in reserve, and following a surprise return to service in the summer of 1977 was sold in 1978. Although Red Funnel have not built a new Voith Schneider ferry or tug since *Vecta* they operated two second-hand Voith Schneider tractor tugs for a number of years for evaluation purposes. However, their two latest tugs are equipped with twin Schottel propulsion units, thus giving a fairly positive indication of the type of propulsion likely to be chosen for replacement ferry tonnage when this becomes due.

Red Funnel was ever the odd man out!

Plate 122. *Norris Castle* started life as a tank loading craft. Similar vessels were employed on an unsuccessful service between Granton and Burntisland on the Forth and could have been used on the Clyde. (K.Abraham)

Plate 123. *Cowes Castle* before 'stretching' and conversion to drive through operation. (K.Adams)

Plate 124. *Netley Castle* at Southampton. The rival 'Red Funnel' route has the longest crossing time to the Island, and passenger facilities are therefore tailored to suit. (J.Hendy)

The Cal-Mac 'Lochs'

It is particularly appropriate and pleasing that this review of *Lymington's* influence on subsequent vessels of the same type should conclude with a group of ferries which in their basic layout are virtually repeats of *Lymington*. A further addition to the Firth of Clyde's increasing number of Voith Schneider ferries, *Isle of Cumbrae,* had joined the CalMac fleet in 1977 and replaced the older twin screw 'Island' class ships on the Largs-Cumbrae Slip service. She was, in effect, a smaller version of the Skye ferries *Kyleakin* and *Lochalsh* and her success prompted CalMac to consider the replacement of the ageing small 'Island' class bow-loading twin-screw craft with a standard design similar to *Isle of Cumbrae,* but with some modifications. The new vessels had to be fully interchangeable and capable of operating any of the company's Clyde and West Highland crossings using the current bow-loaders. Voith Schneider was considered to be the best method of propulsion, but CalMac were also interested in rotatable propeller units on the grounds of reduced cost, and Voith accordingly prepared a Cost Benefit Analysis of twin screw, rotatable propeller and Voith Schneider drives for the company. In view of their experience with Aquamaster rotatable propeller units *(Netley Castle)* CalMac also consulted Red Funnel Steamers, Southampton, whose opinions on the merits of Voith Schneider and rotatable

propeller units largely coincided with those expressed in the Cost Benefit Analysis. Following these investigations CalMac decided on Voith Schneider propulsion, and in late 1981 commissioned Ferguson Ailsa, Port Glasgow, to prepare a design and specification for the new ships. This was eventually put out to tender and resulted in four ferries being ordered from Richard Dunston Ltd., Hessle, for delivery in 1986/87. Since the ferries are considered to be an extension of public transport links they were eligible for a 50% grant from the EEC!

The first two, *Loch Striven* and *Loch Linnhe,* were both allocated to Largs, releasing *Isle of Cumbrae* which was then transferred to the Fishnish-Lochaline route. *Loch Riddon* took over the Colintraive-Rhubodach crossing and the fourth, *Loch Ranza,* operates the Lochranza-Skipness summer only service. The similarity in basic design and layout to *Lymington* can be seen from the accompanying plans and details and it is interesting to note that although rather smaller than the pioneer they have almost twice the power. The full length 2-lane car deck is flanked on each side by passenger saloons, furnished with upholstered seating for 55 on the starboard side and 43 on the port, which also houses a crew mess/galley. Sun decks above the saloons provide open air seating for a further 97 passengers. The benevolence of the EEC is gratefully acknowledged by the display of a gold E on blue background each side of the hull.

Improving the breed

Although the principle of the Voith Schneider propeller remains unchanged a great deal of development work has taken place over the years, resulting in a more robust unit with fewer and simpler working parts. Fabricated and welded components have replaced castings, whilst thrust and gear rings are now of a much greater relative diameter, and these improvements, in conjunction with improved tooth forms and better hardening processes, enable the gears to accept greater loadings than previously. The elimination of sliding surfaces in the kinematics together with pressure lubrication throughout the whole propeller has resulted in far longer periods of operation between surveys. The early uncaged needle roller blade shaft bearings have given way first to caged needles, then plain bushes, and finally to roller bearings, with blade seals having a service life of 8,000-12,000 hours. Indeed, such is the reliability of present day units that some propellers used on highly intensive ferry workings in the U.K. are now running for 50,000 hours (i.e., 10 years) without D.O.T. survey. Hydraulic and electronic control systems have eliminated the awkward runs of mechanical controls, although some owners still prefer the old fashioned skipper-proof and weather-proof system of solid rods, links and gears to the black magic of electronics.

Figure 14. Evolution of the Voith Schneider Propeller.

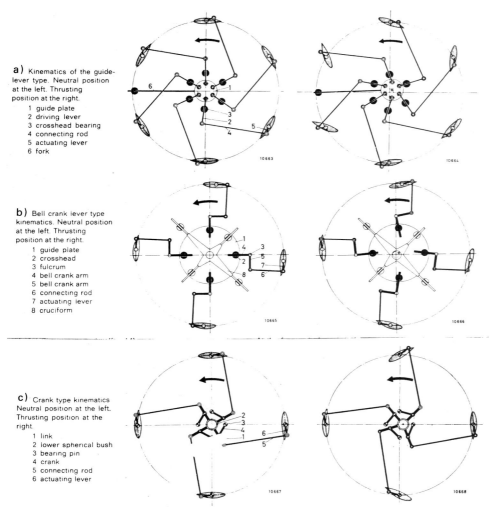

a) Kinematics of the guide-lever type. Neutral position at the left. Thrusting position at the right.
1 guide plate
2 driving lever
3 crosshead bearing
4 connecting rod
5 actuating lever
6 fork

b) Bell crank lever type kinematics. Neutral position at the left. Thrusting position at the right.
1 guide plate
2 crosshead
3 fulcrum
4 bell crank arm
5 bell crank arm
6 connecting rod
7 actuating lever
8 cruciform

c) Crank type kinematics. Neutral position at the left. Thrusting position at the right.
1 link
2 lower spherical bush
3 bearing pin
4 crank
5 connecting rod
6 actuating lever

Plate 125. Calmac's Loch class show the *Lymington* legacy at its best.   (E.C.Goldsworthy & Co.)

73

The Brown Bros. Era

Captain Goldsworthy fully appreciated that in addition to purely commercial applications the Voith Schneider propeller had equal potential for naval use, but all his attempts in pre-war days to interest the Admiralty in this form of propulsion foundered due to the propeller being built in Germany. Two of the shipyards specialising in the construction of small naval craft, Denny's and Thorneycroft's had evinced some interest in building the propeller under licence, and the matter was accordingly put to Voith. Whilst the latter was quite willing to grant a licence for the manufacture of propellers for British and Empire naval craft they were loth to include the potentially lucrative developing commercial market in the deal. Since at the time there was no positive Admiralty interest, or the prospect of obtaining anything other than one or two propellers for naval evaluation in the foreseeable future, the shipyards concerned, not surprisingly, rejected the proposal out of hand. In any case, the grant of a licence for foreign manufacture had to be approved by the German Government, who were far more interested in obtaining foreign currency by export rather than by licence fees, and although Voith did, in fact, make an application, as expected this was turned down. In the event of hostilities between Britain and Germany the owners of British Voith Schneider ships would thus be deprived of spares, supplies and technical advice, a factor which also inhibited wider use of Voith Schneider propulsion in this country, but in spite of the initial rebuffs, Captain Goldsworthy persisted in his efforts to overcome the problem. In July 1939 he was rewarded by the German Government agreeing to let Voith negotiate a licence for the manufacture of Voith Schneider propellers in Britain, for both naval and commercial craft, but by then, of course, it was too late to pursue the matter and no further action was taken.

In addition to the shipyards, Brown Bros., of Edinburgh, steering gear manufacturers had also expressed interest in the licence, and in 1955 a 10-year agreement for Brown Bros., to manufacture Voith Schneider propellers in this country was concluded. Between 1955 and 1965 they built a number of propellers for British ferries, including *Freshwater, Fishbourne (II)* and *Camber Queen*, but relations with Voith were not always as cordial as they might have been. In particular, although they were in close contact with the Admiralty, they appeared to make little effort to assist E.C.Goldsworthy & Co., in the drive to secure an Admiralty order, and their propeller prices were higher than the equivalent Heidenheim built ones. Where an owner obtained tenders from British and Continental yards for a VSP ship the price advantage thus lay with the foreign quotation — to the detriment of Captain Goldsworthy's business. Matters came to a head when a fire at Brown Bros., works seriously disrupted the construction of 3 propellers for PLA tugs, together with a number of smaller propellers for logistic ships and Hong Kong ferries. In the end Voith had to undertake the completion of these units themselves and following this upheaval they decided to terminate the agreement.

In the early years Brown's had not conformed to the specification laid down by Voith and parts for British and German built propellers were not interchangeable. In fairness though, Brown's had latterly instigated some improvements, such as the change-over from blade shaft needle bearings to plain bushes, and a new form of suspension round which the 'G' type propeller was designed became common standard practice. The manufacture of high precision items under licence seems to be fraught with difficulties — one recalls the Voith hydraulic transmissions built by the North British Locomotive Company — which illustrates the absolute devotion and co-operation necessary between all parties to ensure success. The termination of the Brown Bros., licence closed another chapter in the development of the Voith Schneider propeller in this country, during which orders for 97 propellers were received — none of which were from the Admiralty!

Plate 126. Morning Boat. *Sound of Sanda* at Hunters Quay as dawn breaks over the Firth of Clyde. Western Ferries provide by far the best Cowal-Renfrewshire service, sailing from 6am to midnight.
(Alan Brown collection)

Worth a second glance

Unlike the subject of many histories, *Lymington,* as Western Ferries *Sound of Sanda,* is still alive and well and appears likely to remain so for some time. It is hard to predict the future, but her role in the company's fleet may well depend to a large extent on the outcome of charter business at present being negotiated.

The former railway owned Solent ferries have already been returned to private ownership and at the time of writing the bus interests of the STG are also to be privatised. This could be followed by the privatisation of the Caledonian MacBrayne empire and if this should happen the wheel will have then turned full circle.

Drive through operation, whether by double-ended or asymmetrical ferries, has virtually displaced all the previous bow and side-loading methods, and those of the latter which still remain are likely to be converted to drive through in the near future. The Voith Schneider propeller also appears to have a secure future, for in spite of its relatively high initial cost no further system has yet been able to match its overall advantages. By pioneering the combination of double-ended construction with Voith Schneider propulsion *Lymington* is assured of an important and honourable place in the annals of maritime history. In her 50th anniversary year her descendents can be found on the Firth of Clyde, West Highlands, Tyne, Thames, Solent and elsewhere throughout the world, demonstrating the outstanding versatility and manoeuvrability afforded by that mysterious and fascinating device, the Voith Schneider propeller. The car ferry in its many forms has for too long been the Cinderella of coastal, estuarial and river passenger craft, and many interesting and unique vessels have already gone to the breakers, unhonoured and unsung, victims of the road bridge and tunnel lobbies. Whether the quality of life has been enhanced by this 'opening up' of previously remote or difficult of access areas is now becoming a matter of serious debate; what is certain is that no bridge or tunnel can ever replace the charm and romance of a ferry.

The Cinderellas are worth a second glance!

APPENDIX 1

MV LYMINGTON
Log of Voyage from Southampton to Kilmun.

29 March 1974

15.25	Depart Netley Patch
16.03	Calshot Castle (pass,)
16.20	NE Gurnard Buoy (pass)
17.45	Hurst Point Lighthouse (pass)
17.28	North Head Buoy (pass)
19.25	Altered course 260° Compass
24.00	Course 260° Compass

Remarks
All necessary work for voyage to Clyde completed a.m.
Articles opened 11.00
Stores and spares loaded 11.00-13.00
9.00-10.00 Taking bunkers
12.30 Taking fresh water

Weather
Light Northerly winds. Overcast, haze, moderate visibility.

30 March 1974

05.45	Start Point Light abeam
08.50	Eddystone Light abeam
12.36	St Anthony Head abeam starboard
12.38	Pilot on board
12.53	Agent ashore
14.00	Vessel alongside County Berth. Falmouth
15.10	Depart jetty, Falmouth
15.27	Pilot away
15.36	St Anthony Head abeam, port.
19.33	Runnel Stone Buoy abeam
20.05	Longships Lighthouse abeam
24.00	Course 011° Compass

Remarks
14.00-15.10. Stores, fresh water, bunkers taken on at Falmouth County Berth

Weather
Calm. Northerly winds, light. Overcast, moderate visibility.

31 March 1974

24.00	Position by Decca 50 34½ N — 05 46½ W.
00.12	Fog. Visibility 200 yards. DTI Regulations strictly
03.00	Thick fog. Visibility less than ½ length. observed.
09.30	Visibility increased to 2 lengths.
10.35	Smalls abeam starboard
12.00	51 55.7 N — 5 48.4 W.
20.05	Codling Light Vessel abeam. Adjusted course 020°
24.00	025° Compass. Compass

Weather
Light Easterly wind. Slight swell. Overcast.

1 April 1974

05.00	Adjusted course to 029° Compass
07.00	Adjusted course to 040° Compass.
12.00	Course 010° Compass.
12.30	Portpatrick Lighthouse abeam
13.40	Oust Rocks abeam Starboard
17.52	Entered Ayr Harbour
17.57	Approaching berth
18.04	Vessel alongside. Made fast.

Weather
ESE 5. Rough sea. Slight swell. Fine and clear.

2 April 1974

07.37	Vessel leaves berth
07.44	Clear of harbour entrance
12.10	Arrive Hunters Quay Pier
12.30	Depart Hunters Quay
13.00	All fast Kilmun
15.30	Articles closed
17.00	Vessel locked up. Kilmun Pier.

Weather
Moderate Easterly. Cloudy and clear.

APPENDIX 2

Notes on Lymington Motor Carrying Barges (1937)

Tow Boat No 2	Official No 135695 Nett Reg. Tonnage 18 SOUTHAMPTON
Tow Boat No 3	Official No 131786 Nett Reg. Tonnage 19 SOUTHAMPTON
Tow Boat No 4	Official No 16178 Nett Reg. Tonnage 20 SOUTHAMPTON
Tow Boat No 5	Official No 135698 Nett Reg. Tonnage 18 SOUTHAMPTON

All equipped with 13 Life Jackets and 2 Life Buoys.

APPENDIX 3

MV LYMINGTON /SOUND OF SANDA

Crewing

	SR 1938	BR 1970	WF 1988
Master	1	1	1
Mate	1	1	—
Leading Hand	—	1	—
Seamen	3	4	2
Engineer	1	1	1
Greaser	1	1	—
Fireman	—	1	—
Stewards	1	2	—
Stewardesses	2	2	—
Bar Boys	—	2	—
Total	**10**	**16**	**4**

APPENDIX 4

Extract from Log — Monday 27th March 1967

1200 Join ship, singled up and ready to leave.
1245 Alongside south end harbour pier.
1315 Depart south end for Fishbourne, light ship.

			Wind	Sea	Weather	Route
1315	Dep.	Ports.	W-4-5	11	BC	IS
1355	Arr.	Fish.				
1415	Dep.	Fish.	W-5	20	BC	IS
1510	Arr.	Ports.				
1525	Dep.	Ports.	W-5	20	BC	S
1555	Arr.	Ryde				
1615	Dep.	Ryde	W-5	20	C	S
1655	Arr.	Ports.				
1705	Dep.	Ports.	W-5	20	CR	S
1745	Arr.	Ryde				
1810	Dep.	Ryde	W-4-5	20	BC	S
1830	Arr.	Ports.				
1850	Dep.	Ports.	W-4	20	BC	S
2015	Arr.	Fish.				
2030	Dep.	Fish.	W-4	11	BC	S
2120	Arr.	Ports.				

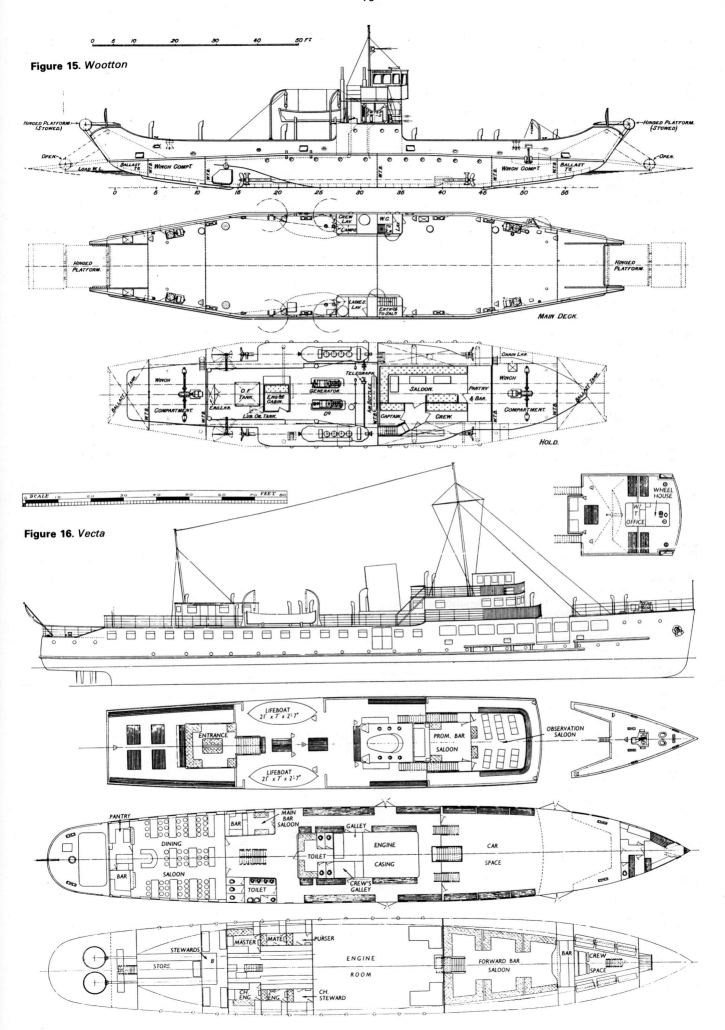

Figure 15. *Wootton*

Figure 16. *Vecta*

76

Figure 17. Proposed design for *Lymington*.

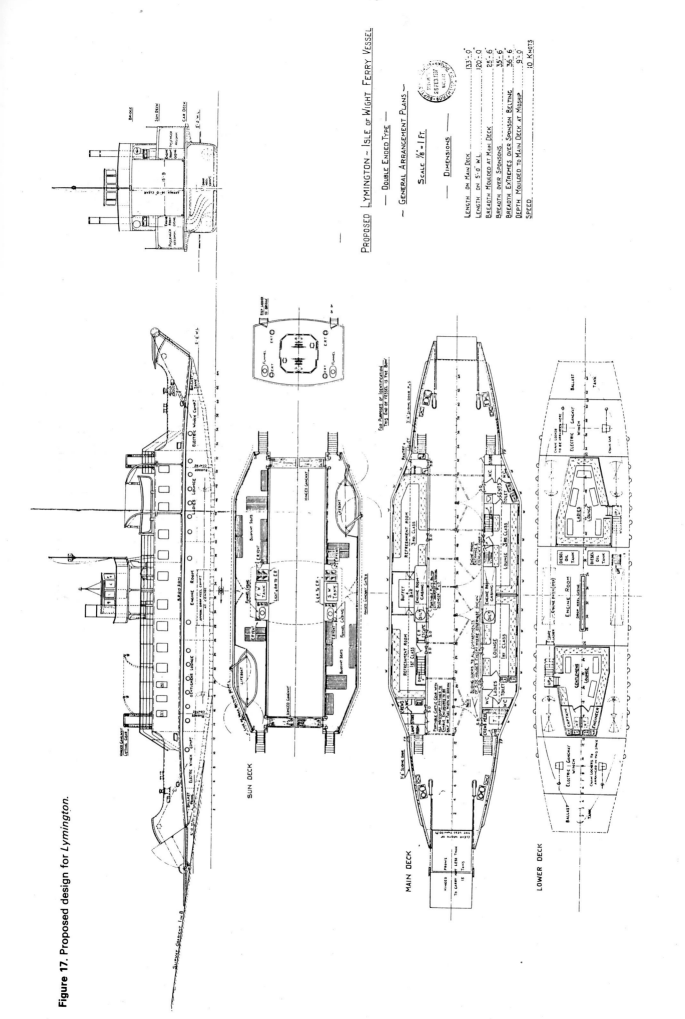

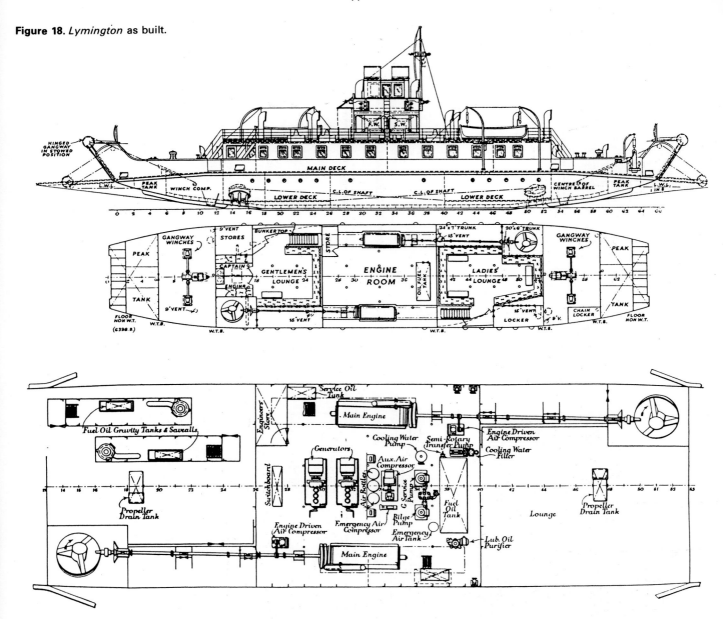

Figure 18. *Lymington* as built.

Figure 19. *Lymington* as fitted with new propellers.

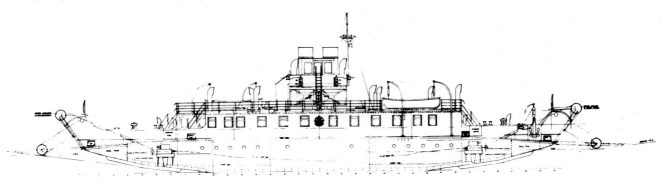

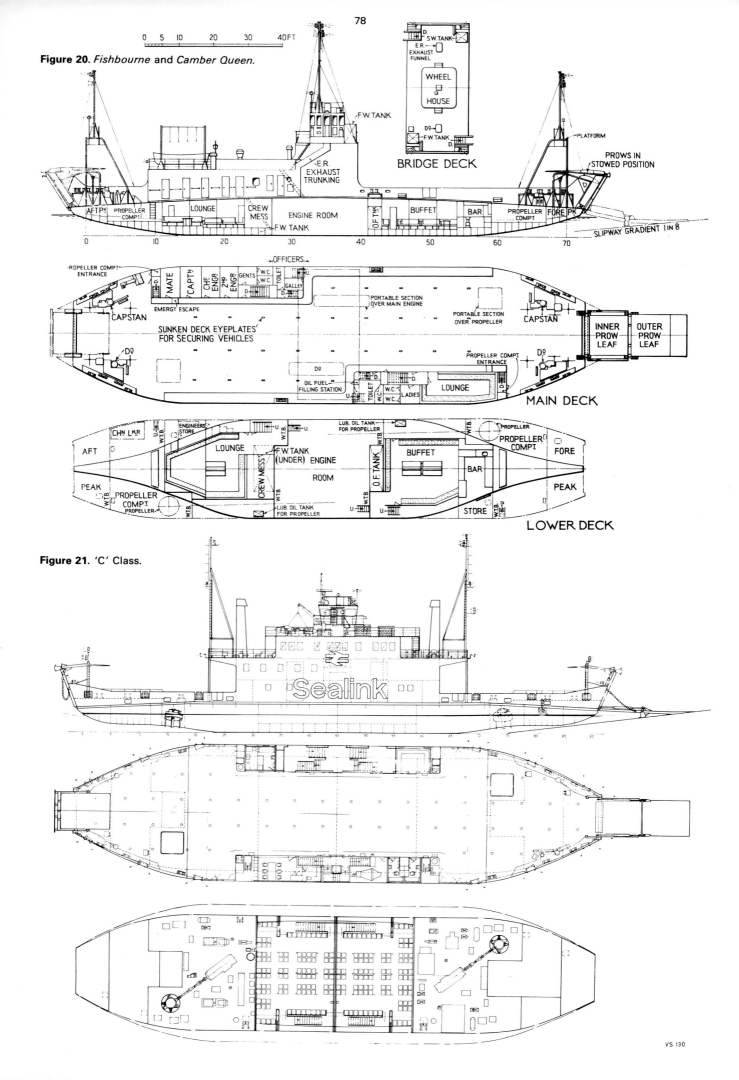

Figure 20. *Fishbourne* and *Camber Queen.*

0 5 10   20   30   40 FT

BRIDGE DECK

S.W. TANK
E.R. EXHAUST FUNNEL
WHEEL HOUSE
F.W. TANK

PLATFORM

PROWS IN STOWED POSITION

F.W. TANK

E.R. EXHAUST TRUNKING

AFT PK   PROPELLER COMPT   LOUNGE   CREW MESS   ENGINE ROOM   O.F. TANK   BUFFET   BAR   PROPELLER COMPT   FORE PK

F.W. TANK

SLIPWAY GRADIENT 1 IN 8

0   10   20   30   40   50   60   70

OFFICERS

PROPELLER COMPT ENTRANCE

MATE   CAPTN   CHF ENGR   2ND ENGR   GENTS   W.C.   W.C.   TOILET   GALLEY

EMERGY ESCAPE

CAPSTAN

SUNKEN DECK EYEPLATES FOR SECURING VEHICLES

PORTABLE SECTION OVER MAIN ENGINE

PORTABLE SECTION OVER PROPELLER

CAPSTAN

INNER PROW LEAF   OUTER PROW LEAF

OIL FUEL FILLING STATION

TOILET   W.C.   W.C.   LADIES   LOUNGE

PROPELLER COMPT ENTRANCE

MAIN DECK

CHN LKR   ENGINEERS STORE

LOUNGE

F.W. TANK (UNDER)   ENGINE ROOM

CREW MESS

LUB. OIL TANK FOR PROPELLER

O.F. TANK

BUFFET

PROPELLER

PROPELLER COMPT

AFT   PEAK

BAR

FORE   PEAK

PROPELLER COMPT   PROPELLER

LUB. OIL TANK FOR PROPELLER

STORE

LOWER DECK

Figure 21. 'C' Class.

Sealink

VS 130

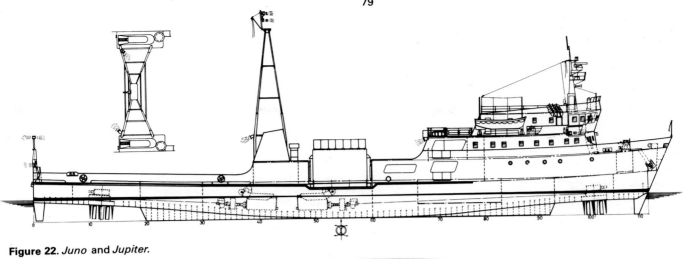

Figure 22. *Juno* and *Jupiter*.

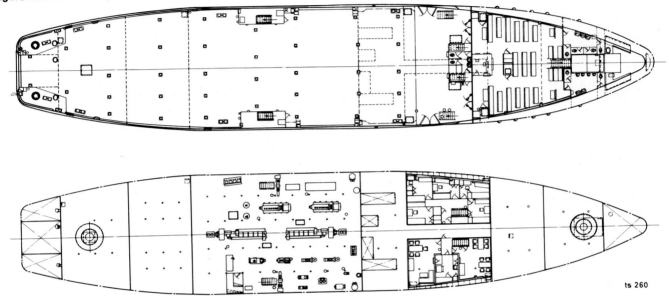

ts 260

Figure 23. *St Catherine*.

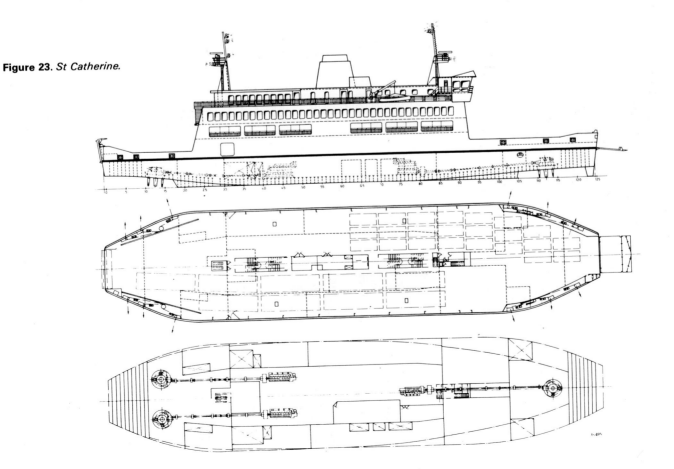

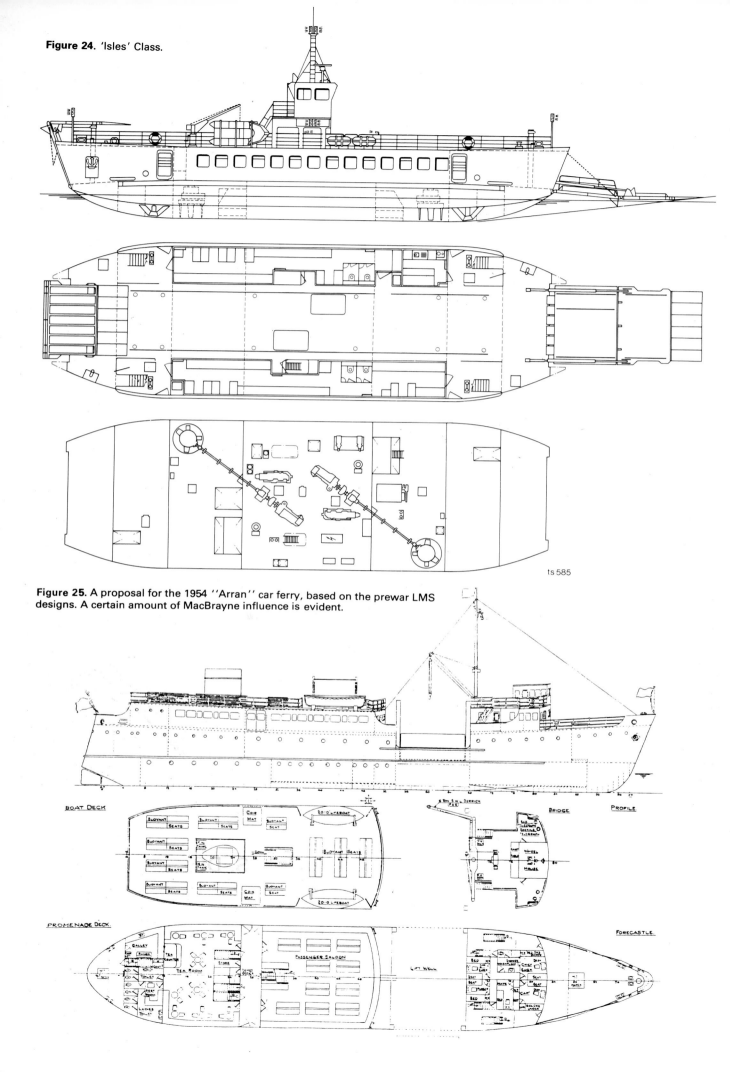

Figure 24. 'Isles' Class.

ts 585

Figure 25. A proposal for the 1954 ''Arran'' car ferry, based on the prewar LMS designs. A certain amount of MacBrayne influence is evident.